QUANTUM GOVERNANCE

QUANTUM GOVERNANCE

Rewiring the Foundation of Public Policy

By

Fadi Farra
Whiteshield

With

Christopher Pissarides
London School of Economics

United Kingdom – North America – Japan
India – Malaysia – China

Emerald Publishing Limited
Emerald Publishing, Floor 5, Northspring, 21-23 Wellington Street, Leeds LS1 4DL.

First edition 2023

Copyright © 2023 Fadi Farra.
Published under exclusive licence by Emerald Publishing Limited.

Reprints and permissions service
Contact: www.copyright.com

British Library Cataloguing in Publication Data
A catalogue record for this book is available from the British Library

ISBN: 978-1-83753-779-2 (Print)
ISBN: 978-1-83753-778-5 (Online)
ISBN: 978-1-83753-780-8 (Epub)

Printed and bound by CPI Group (UK) Ltd, Croydon, CR0 4YY

INVESTOR IN PEOPLE

A ma famille
—Fadi Farra

CONTENTS

ABOUT THE AUTHORS

The book has been published by Whiteshield, a global public policy and strategy firm originating in the Harvard and OECD communities that specialises in delivering innovation and tangible policy reforms to a portfolio of leaders from governments, international organisations and Fortune 500 companies.

The book has been developed under the leadership of Fadi Farra, Founder and Managing Partner, Whiteshield, Former Lecturer at the Harvard Kennedy School of Government, and Former Head of Unit, OECD. Fadi Farra has more than twenty years of experience in strategy consulting and policy advisory globally, including industrial and innovation policies, microeconomics, private sector development and competitiveness policies. He is the author of numerous publications related to innovation, competitiveness and industrial policy, and a regular commentator in leading world media. As founder of Whiteshield, Fadi Farra received distinguished awards for his outstanding achievements in the field of consulting. In 2019, he was honoured with the Global Leaders in Consulting Award with Excellence in Innovation. Additionally, Consulting Magazine recognised him as one of the Top 25 Consultants in 2021 for his outstanding contributions to the public sector. Fadi's expertise is widely acknowledged, as evidenced by his chairmanship of the Global Agenda Council on the Future of Manufacturing Council at the World Economic Forum. He is also a frequent commentator in global media.

Sir Christopher A. Pissarides FBA is a British-Cypriot economist. He is the School Professor of Economics & Political Science and Regius Professor of Economics at the London School of Economics, and Professor of European Studies at the University of Cyprus. His research focuses on topics of macroeconomics, notably labour, economic growth, and economic policy. In 2010, he was awarded the Nobel Prize in Economics, jointly with Peter A. Diamond and Dale Mortensen, "for their analysis of markets with theory of search frictions". He is also a Special Advisor and Director at Whiteshield. He served as the chairman of the National Economy Council of the Republic of Cyprus during the country's financial crisis in 2012 and resigned to focus on his academic work at the end of 2014.

The larger contributing team includes several Whiteshield employees including Amira Bensebaa, Principal; and Elena Balter, Senior Economist. Amira holds a M.Sc. in public and private management from SciencesPo and HEC, Paris, France and was instrumental in drafting various sections of the book and coordinating the consolidation process. Elena's outstanding skills in econometric and statistical analysis were substantial to the modelling and quantitative analysis that support the research and inform many of the book's recommendations.

FOREWORD

David E. Bell

I am a marketing professor. A lot has changed in my field in recent years. Now marketers try to influence your buying behaviour by sending you **personalised** ads through social media. The 'personalisation' is automated because it is possible to track how you responded to previous ads, when you bought, when you didn't and so on. Advertisers know exactly how effective their campaigns are. They also know that people are highly influenced, not so much by the marketers themselves, but by people they trust. In the old days, these **influencers** were friends or neighbours. Now they are more likely to be people who have developed a following online and who can influence their followers on what to buy. Advertisers now try to co-opt these **Key Opinion Leaders** by courting their opinion or, more simply, paying them a fee. In China, there are highly watched online 'talk shows' where the guests are celebrity KOLs.

There are so many other changes in our lives brought about by digitalisation that it's hard to keep up. Cryptocurrencies like Bitcoin soon could hold more value than all of the world's gold. This in a handful of years, and all due to digitisation.

Politics is also not what it was. 'Smoke-filled rooms' are long gone. The public used to find out, if they did at all, about who voted for what, long after the fact. Now, every politician's votes, statements and blunders are known at once. The amazing political ascent of Donald Trump may have been due to his constant tweeting: talking directly, constantly, to his supporters, an example few seem to be copying.

There is a common lesson in these transformations. It is that we should no longer think of people in terms of demographics, like the middle class, the left or the baby boomers, but as individuals, because we now can, and we should.

Public policy has not got that message. Governments still make investments, launch programmes and urge the citizenry as if people came in blocs, often just one bloc. This book is a call to action to rethink how we do public policy. The authors call it **Quantum Governance** to highlight the central role of the individual.

Their proposal is not just a think piece. They have carried out a systematic analysis dissecting public policy effectiveness across most countries of the world. They have identified a number of fixable issues:

1. Governments tend to launch programmes without enough regard for the **absorptive capacity** of the people. If you have your thirteen-year-old listen to online college lectures, it won't do any good because the child doesn't yet have the capacity to take it in. People come in all shapes and sizes, with respect to how they process information, their capabilities and their needs. Public spending that exceeds the absorptive capacity of the nation is a waste of money. Some countries may need to invest in building, or at least measuring, absorptive capacity.

2. Public policies interact with one another, yet they are often supervised, funded and monitored as if they are independent. These days we can figure out how they interact and plan accordingly. The authors present a periodic table' illustrating how policies may be seen as interrelated.

3. Companies are increasingly turning to the concept of a Balanced Scorecard to assess their condition and to measure progress. By analogy, countries need to consider how they measure their nations' balance sheet: how well off are they? Age-old measures like GDP and Balance of Payments don't capture the cumulative welfare of individuals, their potential or their quality of life. These measures were invented when data was hard to come by and never did a good job handling the intangibles of value creation.

The authors propose a new equation for understanding the effectiveness of public policies in which government actions and capabilities should be in balance with the **absorptive capacity** of the people. In marketing, we have a concept of the customer journey: a person begins the journey never having heard of a product, then they become familiar with it, then they develop an opinion, then they decide whether to buy or not. These journeys are highly idiosyncratic and highly dependent on **influencers** and **cultural norms.** In the public policy arena, one speech from the White House cannot possibly transform the thinking of many.

On the other side of the equation, governments should introduce good policies, more accurately **a good mix of policies** and implement the policies **efficiently**. However, more than that, they need to have the capability to **persuade** and lead. In today's partisan world, half of a country's people may not find the leadership credible.

There is much more detail to be found in theory and in the book. I think you would agree that in this digital age where breathtaking change is happening in almost every facet of our lives, the way in which governments manage our quality of life is ready for a makeover.

David E. Bell
Professor at Harvard Business School

PREFACE

Where do we stand as a global community in terms of development? Some might argue that before COVID-19, things were looking up, economies were fully recovering from the 2008 Financial Crisis, exponential technological progress was holding the promise of accelerated growth, and according to the most optimistic analysis, there was the promise of better jobs and a net creation of new ones. Low- and middle-income countries were achieving noticeable progress in poverty reduction, and the win-win scenario of green economies combining a lower environmental footprint and higher innovation and growth was depicted as a reachable and attractive future.

If we look closer at key facts, the myth of the great acceleration might be just that: a myth. Economists have been grappling with the productivity paradox where the technological miracle is not fulfilling its economic promises, productivity growth being at its lowest historical levels. Displays of social unrest have been accelerating all around the world with the emergence of several large-scale movements, be it the Arab Spring, Occupy Wall Streets, climate strikes, or the Black Lives Matter movement. Combined with the rise of populism, this denotes the erosion of social cohesion and strong opposition to the status quo and our traditional societal paradigms. Finally, the United Nations cannot repeat this enough; the world is overwhelmingly not on track to achieve Sustainable Development Goals. COVID-19 is set to make things worse with implications far beyond the short-term impact we are seeing. What started as a health crisis has since evolved into a deep, economic, social and political one. A crisis threatening to reverse thirty years of achievements in poverty reduction, double the number of people facing starvation, set us back in the transition towards greener economies as short-term priorities prevail and worsen our monetary infrastructure as central banks around the world engage in perpetual money printing to try and contain the socio-economic damages.

However, there is a silver lining linked to our human tendency to revisit fundamental questions in a crisis context. Indeed, the crisis offers a window of opportunity, a small time-bubble during which people are collectively drawn to understanding what went wrong, asking what it was that brought us here, and considering changing our business-as-usual practices, frameworks and paradigms. We invite the readers to engage in this long-overdue process to avoid wasting this opportunity. By bringing attention to fundamental questions, we set out to identify the constants of development, the key drivers of changes across the space–time continuum of our societies.

This journey led us to the conclusion that we need a new policy framework. One that does not rely on linear mechanistic thinking, and one that is not constrained by a reductionist approach to the world, segregating realities into artificial dichotomies and abstract silos: the economy, the private sector, the civil society, education policy and innovation. One that is aligned with real-world complexity and one that takes the individual as the main unit of analysis and action. For far too long, we relied on a misleading vision of human beings, portraying them as simple atomistic agents. We need to bring back the individuals in their full complexity to the change formula. For any social organisation is nothing else but a network of interacting individuals and no public policy can deliver impact or progress in development goals without an impact on individuals' lives. People are the key conversion factor. Their ability to absorb public policies and convert them into tangible achievements is the only real driver of change and should be at the heart of our development reflections.

**It is time to centre our actions around the
quantum unit of the social world: the citizen.**

Fadi Farra,
Founder and Managing Partner, Whiteshield,
Former Lecturer at the Harvard Kennedy School of Government, and
Former Head of Unit, OECD.
Christopher A. Pissarides,
Special Advisor and Director, Whiteshield and
Nobel Laureate in Economic Sciences

Introduction

REWIRING THE FOUNDATIONS OF PUBLIC POLICY

CHANGE IS EVERYWHERE; WHERE IS CHANGE? THE GREAT PARADOX OF OUR TIMES

'We have entered a new era', 'we are stuck in business-as-usual and need a paradigm change'. Yes, these mainstream narratives at least ring a bell and at most sound cliché because, in the wake of a new decade in the 21st century, we have been hearing them for years, sometimes even from the same individuals, be it policymakers, international organisations, media, experts, business leaders or average citizens. They both coexist in the realm of shared sentiments about our times. However, they are paradoxical. How can we witness structural and radical transformations at a pace that some say has never been this fast, and yet share this impression of global inertia, a sense that we are still operating under the same frameworks? How can reiterated conscious calls for structural change remain just that, calls? If we had indeed entered a new era, why do we grapple so much with defining it?

A Narrative of Progress...

The ways our lives, economies and societies have changed over the past few decades have been carefully and extensively documented and analysed. These changes are intrinsically related to technological progress and its wide-ranging implications. Saying that we as individuals have witnessed a radical shift in our daily lives, that we have more information, or data, at our fingertips than ever before, that technology has opened up, and continues to open up, endless opportunities materialized in new ways of working, trading, communicating or learning is simply stating the obvious. Claiming that these changes are not confined to the micro-scale level but are just as prominent in the ways our societies and our economies work has long ceased to be groundbreaking news. Talk about the knowledge economy as the foregone path we are headed towards started as early as the 1960s with American management consultant Peter Drucker's famous 'landmarks of tomorrow'. The hype around the Fourth Industrial Revolution (4IR) somehow already feels outdated, even before its full materialisation, due to how intensively it has been relayed over the past few years. We are all familiar with the narrative that we are transitioning to capitalism without capital, that the key input of our economies has shifted from capital to intangible assets, to talent, data and knowledge, and that production modes are changing from hierarchical to spontaneous and collaborative. Far from us to paint here a utopian picture of a digital era, but the task at hand is not to judge whether it is a positive or negative change, simply to state that the mainstream narrative around progress (or the new era) is a justified and widely recognised one. While prominent, technology-related change does not even hold a monopoly over this narrative. From the enacted change in the world order to demographic trends, to climate change, and corporate and development sustainability, the wide range of transformational mega-trends we are facing corroborates the narrative that we have entered a new era.

... Or Inertia?

The other side of the story is stagnation, the sense that we are locked in a status quo that we have been calling to challenge and change in vain. This narrative might be driven by three related observations.

The first revolves around the scale and the pace of change described above. Technology is changing our lives, but can we really make that statement when half of the global population does not have access to that technology, the famous digital divide, and even more to the skills and capabilities required to use and leverage it? Can we really pretend to have entered the era of the digital economy if we are only focusing on developed economies? Can we claim that 4IR is our new reality when only a handful of companies have adopted its technologies while most countries still need to catch up with the third automation wave? Since exponential technological progress is not materialising in productivity gains as it is supposed to, then radically new production modes might still be niche segments at the hands of a few visionaries.

The second observation relates to our frameworks: the game might have changed, but its rules did not. The new economic paradigms of the digital age were supposed to shift the focus to networks, to granularity, yet their strongest current manifestations are tech giants, monopolies bigger than ever witnessed in modern times. Collaborative management frameworks are praised and set to be the new norm, yet the top-down hierarchy of command-and-control is still profoundly rooted everywhere, from administrations to the average corporation. Talent and knowledge are said to be the new capital, and we still measure talent as a cost rather than a value. Corporate sustainability has been embraced, but one line of the triple-bottom line still matters far more than others, and prices are still incomplete, not capturing environmental and social impacts. The Sustainable Development Agenda has been adopted by 193 countries but narrow-sided metrics such as gross domestic product (GDP) or unemployment rates still shape the dominant policy paradigm.

The third observation is the recognised need for change confronted by the inability to enact it with the recurrent yet unfulfilled calls for a paradigm shift. These calls tend to intensify after each disruption; each crisis is meant to remind us that there are repetitive failures and a status quo to be challenged. We have seen it with the 2008 Financial Crisis and the COVID-19 crisis which generated converging voices towards the need for a 'great reset', a 'building back better' movement.

So how do we explain the paradox? Why do we feel that structural and rapid change is ubiquitous and yet still observe stagnation, still operate under the same frameworks and vainly repeat that we need to break out of business-as-usual? Four hypotheses can help us explain this.

1. We have not entered a new era. What we are witnessing are incremental changes within the same paradigm rather than a structural leap towards a new step. The challenge is to reconcile new and increasing external constraints with the fundamentals of this lasting paradigm.

2. 'The old world is dying, and the new world struggles to be born.' Simply put, we are in a transitionary period, and every transition comes with its challenges and its paradoxes. The full shift to a new era is set and unavoidable but will require more time. Half a century from now,

the hindsight that can only come from studying History will help us uncover how all the pieces of the puzzle fit together to fully enable the emergence of this new world.

3. Looking at the world with outdated goggles: the paradox highlighted is only an apparent one. In reality, if the scale of change does not appear as great as we would expect from entering a new step, it is simply because we are still measuring it with old tools and methodologies. We need a new cognitive infrastructure that is able to accurately depict and analyse these evolutions.

4. It is not about the time or pace of change; it is about convergence. The paradox is a real one and is due to a divergence in operating frameworks. We no longer have a common policy language and a common direction. While parts of our societal systems have indeed engaged in structural transformations, others are still locked in an outdated paradigm, and our global transition's faith is not yet final precisely because of this lack of convergence. The real acceleration can be seen in increasing tensions arising from this divergence.

Relatively strong arguments can be made for each hypothesis, but we are interested in exploring the last one. What are the sources of this divergence in our systems' direction and operating frameworks?

POLICY CYNICISM: THE GREAT DISILLUSION

Understanding the lack of convergence causing the paradoxes of our era requires looking at the set of institutions, rules, laws and frameworks precisely supposed to enable movement towards a common direction in our societies: public policies. When doing so, one can only notice a strong link between the status quo, inertia sentiment and another common mainstream narrative of our times: failures of public policy.

The second half of the 20th century saw the beginnings of a trend known as political cynicism, a general disaffection with politics from institutions to governments, their decisions, the political process in general and the word 'politics' itself, which became heavily charged with a negative connation. We argue that this political cynicism has further expanded during the past few decades to become policy cynicism. It is no longer simply a negative image of policymakers as being corrupt or prioritising self-interest, it is also the notion that the public policy world is too slow, at odds with the agility required for our times, and that policy failures are abundant. Regardless of the actual quality of public policies put in place, regardless of the intentions of policymakers, there is a growing perception that it is simply not enough to tackle pressing and complex challenges. The sentence 'why isn't the government doing anything about this' has become so common that it is impossible to separate the inertia narrative from policy failures. While the challenges and expectations from public policy are rising considerably, its capabilities to respond to them are simply stagnating. The normalisation of this loss of faith in public policy is itself an issue but also just a symptom of a model running out of breath, unable to drive convergence in a critical period of structural transformations.

CLOSED SYSTEMS: THE GREAT CHALLENGE

US President Ronald Reagan's 'Government is not the solution to our problem. Government is the problem' famously embodies this normalised disillusion with policymaking. At the same time, how this statement has come to be used over the following decade, emerging from the end of the cold war ideologies, hints at the answer as to why policy systems have not been able to adapt and transform in tandem with changing socio-economic contexts, challenges and development goals. The reason is that policymaking became jailed in a closed debate: 'government is good, we need more government' vs 'government is bad, we need less of it' when actually, to begin with, we should have been questioning the core nature of government, and what type of government we needed. Thus, we are focusing on finding answers without considering the option that we are not asking the right questions. This is the closed system challenge.

Answers are a finite game; they are played within the boundaries, rules and expectations. But questions, fundamental questions, they play with the boundaries, they define them. And a closed system is one that fails to ask fundamental questions and persists in looking for answers within the same boundaries. Closed systems are thus inherently incapable of self-regeneration or spontaneous adaptation and are not resilient. The most dangerous aspect of a system is to become so entrenched in assumptions raised to the standard of absolute truth that it is no longer capable of real change, of admitting those assumptions are not valid anymore; that is when thinking becomes ideology.

This book gives answers, answers as to how policymaking in our times can change to avoid the path that all closed systems ended up facing in History: perishing. But our objective is not to replace a closed debate with another one but precisely to open it, to set a framework where systematic questioning is built in, a framework that revives the importance of questions. What does development mean? What drives civilisational change, from the first urban settlements in Mesopotamia to the creation of the first green smart cities? From the first agricultural exploitations to the knowledge economy? How did we, as a human community, build the world as we know it, and what will define the next steps of our journey on earth? All of these are fundamental questions and asking fundamental questions has long gone out of fashion for individuals in general and, let alone in the policymaking sphere; questions without easy solutions; questions that are too big to answer; questions that are too subversive to normalise. Our objective is to bring them back.

Public policy is dominated by 'how' questions: How do we develop? How do we create more jobs? How do we eradicate poverty? How do we use taxes to reduce inequalities? How do we fight climate change? Most current policy questions are 'how' questions. Why should we be concerned about that? For two main reasons. First, the answers to 'how' questions are stories of change which are bound to evolve. The risk is to stop questioning them and take them as universal truths. Second, 'how' questions tend to lead to reasoning by analogy: we attempt to find the answer in what was successfully done in the past or in what is successfully being done in other countries or other regions. The two risks combined means tackling changing problems with outdated or irrelevant strategies. The lens that we should use is 'what' questions: What is development? What is a public policy? What is a job? Starting a labour committee meeting with 'What is a job?' instead of 'How do we create more jobs?' might sound foolish, yet it is the only question enabling us to account for the structural and profound changes of labour markets and the debates around the future of work.

FINDING THE CONSTANTS IN THE SPACE–TIME CONTINUUM

So how can we use fundamental questions to ensure our policy systems remain open? How can we embed this level of critical thinking and reflexivity in our frameworks so that change does not become explicable only in the rear-view mirror of History, so that envisioning and achieving present and future changes is possible? We need to shift the focus from narratives of change (answers to 'how' questions) to characters of change or intemporal change factors (answers to 'what' questions). In other words, our analytical frameworks need to be based on variables that have always and will always be the drivers of change because they are inherent to it.

To illustrate this point, let us introduce here a small time-travel thought experiment taking us through three stories of change.

Tiberius in Rome, Circa 125 BC

Tiberius is one of those few individuals whose mere birth is said to destine them to greatness. He knows History will never forget his grandfather, the man who liberated Rome, the great Republic, from the threat of a fierce enemy: Hannibal. He knows that as his father he will go on to serve in the most respected institutions of the Republic. He knows that shining in public life is what everyone expects from him. The standards are high; election as a Tribune will not be enough for a family whose men held the tradition of serving as Consul, the highest political position in the Republic.

That year, Tiberius had taken his first steps in the public realm. Sent to fight for the Republic in Spain, his army ended up being captured despite all reasonable efforts. Emboldened by the stories of the great men before him, he decided that leaving his people captured was not an option and undertook negotiations for a peace treaty, a task that, despite his prominent social position, was still above his power as a debutant. Nonetheless, and helped by his outstanding oratory skills and a confidence that only men of his breeding could display, he managed to come away with a winning treaty, leaving no man behind while barely conning to the enemy.

He returned to Rome confident he made the right choice, expecting to be praised for it. You can imagine his surprise when, instead, the Senate called the treaty a disgrace because Romans could not afford to stoop to negotiations to surrender. Talks about undoing the treaty started among Patricians (the aristocrats of Rome) and leaders of the Senate.

Tiberius's confusion turned to outrage. He had saved the lives of tens of thousands of Roman citizens. That had to be worth it even if the soldiers were not Patricians but Plebeians of lower social stature. After all, weren't Romans supposed to be one, unified under the greatest Republic of all? Wasn't his duty, as the descendent of men of virtue and morals, to put the well-being and livelihood of his 'weaker' fellow citizens above all considerations of pride?

However, Tiberius ends up seeing the misadventure as a blessing in disguise. The rumours about undoing the negotiations spread and incited the legions of the soldiers and families he saved to rally around him. Confronted with popular pressure, Senators gave up on their project but could neither forget nor forgive. It was the first time soldiers of the Republic had displayed greater allegiance to an individual rather than the Republic's greatest, most respected institution. It was the first time that citizens of Rome had taken politics out of the institutional sphere, out of the hands of the individuals supposed to represent them and back into their own hands. They were glimpsing a shift in the core of Roman values.

Tiberius knows he has made enemies among the Senators, but he also knows that giving up on his political ambitions is not an option; that will be the greatest disgrace of all for his family's legacy. Before these events, Tiberius could not have imagined being criticised by Patricians and praised by Plebeians. But he decides to lean into this new position and to run for Plebs Tribune. This implies getting to know the concerns of his future constituency, for his own were rather small to non-existent. His family-owned land and houses, their wealth increasing over the years, political life was his destiny, and despite this plot twist, he always knew his future was guaranteed. He knew Plebs and citizens of lower social stature did not have the same life, but he was far from knowing how much their lives had deteriorated over the recent past. His new allies tell him life was much kinder to their fathers and grandfathers.

After his grandfather defeated Hannibal, Romans of all classes participated in rebuilding Italy, which was financially fruitful for all. Generations before them had started borrowing money from the richest to bid on contracts for various rebuilding projects. The less fortunate could work while the rich collected interest from the loans. But over the years, benefits slowed down for the poor while the wealthy kept getting wealthier. Tiberius' allies tell him they are ashamed. They know how their parents lived and they too are capable of the same hard work and strive for the same standards, but have to settle for less. They tell him it is getting worse and worse. While summoned to fight for the Republic far from their homes, they would leave their lands and come back to find them damaged but they were also confronted with far greater competition from big landowners with armies of enslaved people. Most of them would end up selling their land and moving to Rome, struggling to find work and pursue a decent life.

Tiberius decides to revive an old land reform proposed by Tribunes long before him, but which never came to be because of the Senate's opposition. The reform aims at setting a limit for public land that individuals can use and the redistribution of the excess land to Romans who do not have any. His proposition is once again opposed by the Senate, claiming that political institution's role is to defend the values and morals of the Republic, not legislate on financial matters beneath them.

But Tiberius, driven by his own ambitions and this new cause, is determined not to give up. He initiates a whole narrative about the issue, drawing on the same values the Senate pretends to defend, 'The wild beasts that roam over Italy,' he says, 'have every one of them a cave or lair to lurk in. However, the men who fight and die for Italy enjoy the common air and light but nothing else. Houseless and homeless, they wander about with their wives and children, and though they are styled masters of the world, they have not a single clod of earth that is their own.'

His support among the Plebs keeps getting stronger. One step at a time, he is emboldened to break rules which are at the heart of the Republic. These are not explicit rules but unspoken ones, so deeply rooted in the Republic's history that no one thinks they can ever be transgressed. Then comes Tiberius. Tiberius defies the Senate with the help of his army of supporters, not violently but audaciously. He sidesteps the Senate and passes the land reform through the Plebeian Assembly. Tiberius goes on to find money through popular support to fund the execution of his reform when the Senate refuses to allocate any budget to it.

Tiberius ran for Tribune after his first term, again not an illegal act, but certainly an unprecedented one. Throughout all these breachings of unspoken Roman rules of conduct, Tiberius never incited violence but was always supported by a concerningly large base backing his every move. For his Senator enemies, standing for re-election was the final straw. For the first time in 300 years of the Roman Republic, they decided to resort to violence and assassinate Tiberius.

The Republic did not end with this event, and it continued to survive for another century. However, this was a dangerous precedent which introduced into the Roman collective memory the possibility of challenging informal institutions, unspoken rules, and strongly held beliefs, and to use violence in the political scene. It opened the door to a century of violence and civil war. It paved the way for Julius Caesar and the fall of the Republic.

Camille and Robespierre in France, 1789

Camille, Paris, 12 July 1789
Camille is not a skilled orator. He could not go through a whole sentence without the unfortunate habit of stuttering. Sadly, it is ironic for a man whose livelihood depends on delivering persuasive speeches in court. But today, on the 12th of July 1789, surrounded by a Parisian crowd in the gardens of the Palais-Royal, he feels empowered by a strange, almost mystic energy. He jumps onto one of the tables of the Café de Foy and addresses the people. He is not prepared for it, but words start flowing instinctively. Swept away by the power of the moment, he is almost audience to his own speech. 'To arms! to arms! . . .' he exhorts the crowd, 'At least they will not take me alive, and I am ready to die a glorious death! I can only meet with a single misfortune, and that would be to see France in bondage'.

Earlier that day, rumour has it that Necker was dismissed from his functions as Chief Minister, news that prompted fear, chaos, and a call to arms. 'The exile of a single man had become a public calamity.' It was not about the man; it was about what he represented. A source of hope, hope that much-needed reforms would go through, hope that the Monarchy was ready to listen to the Third Estate, and hope that the newly proclaimed National Assembly would be able to convey and defend the interests of the people. That hope was starting to shatter away. The widespread anticipation and optimism that the revival of the Estates-General had sparked gave way to desperation and fear. A fear that nobles would not allow it, that the king would side with them and that the people would pay the price for challenging the existing order.

Camille reminds the crowd that: 'the Nation had asked for Necker to be retained, and he has been driven out!' 'Could you be more insolently flouted?' he asks. 'After such an act, they will dare anything, and they may perhaps be planning and preparing a Saint Bartholomew massacre of patriots for this very night!'. Camille is only saying out loud what the people are already thinking. Necker is the only popular minister, famous for his social and tax reforms, his attempts to increase transparency around the public budget, his efforts to supply the country with grain when famine loomed, and his support for doubling the representation of the Third Estate. To the people, his dismissal sounded the death knell of change and could only be a precursor to famine, bankruptcy and civil war. Thus, arms seemed like the last resort, and for arms, they went looking.

Well into the night, Camille starts writing. He feels the next few days will be unprecedented, groundbreaking and he ought to document them. He also feels the Parisian crowd is in dire need of exaltation and ideals to sustain the energy, to help picture a freer, fairer and brighter future. 'La France Libre' (Free France) is in the making. A pamphlet to divide and unite. The dividing is easy enough. Anger against the current order, against the privileges, against the nobles and everything they embody, is well engrained among the Parisian and the provincial crowds alike. Social and economic despair had already turned political. The uniting around new values and new ideals is harder. Camille is not lacking in inspiration, from his days perusing the philosophy of antiquity at the Lycée Louis le Grand to heated readings of Rousseau, Voltaire and Montesquieu in secret meetings. Popular sovereignty, natural rights and the nation, Camille raises as the guiding principles of 'La France Libre'.

Robespierre, Versailles, 14 July 1789
The constituent Assembly is a few days old. The initial excitement had left Robespierre with great fear over its future. Rumours were spreading left and right about the king and the nobles' manoeuvres to stop the deputies. Mirabeau's speech on the looming threat of a military retaliation is still resonating. The news of Necker's dismissal is certainly not a good sign. Paris is grounding. The Assembly is standing on shaking ground; Robespierre knows it. Its self-proclaimed legitimacy, so far reluctantly accepted by the king, could shift overnight to an outright rebellion, an illegitimate usurpation, a treason. His mail of the day includes a letter from his old classmate and dear friend Camille. Robespierre hurries to open it, eager to find out about the latest news from Paris.

'We took the Bastille.' 'We killed its governor.' 'France is free.' 'The will of the people shall prevail.' He could almost hear Camille's voice proclaiming these words. These exciting yet terribly frightening words. He runs to break the news to his fellow deputies. In Versailles, the heavy silence, the palpable tension, the consternated looks – everything says they know and share his fears. Debating among themselves is useless. The fate of the Assembly is going to be decided today, but not by them. They are not ready for a confrontation. The people are not ready for it either. All they can do is wait, wait for 'His' reaction, a reaction that will shape the very meaning of this event. The king sees the 14th of July as a terrible affront to his authority, an act of insubordination and as such a discredit to their newly claimed authority. Louis XVI decides to call back Necker and remove its troops. What could have killed the Assembly prematurely becomes the very source of legitimacy that the deputies so desperately need. The 14th of July becomes an act of popular sovereignty, and the Assembly becomes the legitimate representative of that sovereignty. The will of the people shall prevail indeed. These would be Robespierre's words writing back to Camille that same day and these would be his words a month later announcing the adoption of the Declaration of the Rights of Man and of the Citizen.

Miremba in Davos, 2020

One year ago, Miremba really could not have predicted spending her twenty-first birthday in Switzerland, thousands of miles away from her home and family in Kampala, camping in a tent in sub-zero temperatures while the most powerful leaders and companies gathered for the annual World Economic Forum meeting. She had never heard of Davos until a few months ago. She read up about it in preparation for this experience. The elite, the exorbitant financial cost, the private jets, the parties, and the speeches, all of it, could not have felt more distant from her life. Nevertheless, she is here to start a dialogue and is determined to keep an open mind. Looking back at the journey that led her here, she cannot help but feel optimistic.

Her beginnings as a self-identified climate activist date to about two years before. Unprecedented heatwaves were raging in Uganda, significantly impacting daily life, destroying crops, pushing farmers further into poverty and increasing famine throughout the country. Discussions with older family members about the unprecedented heat levels pushed her to investigate their origins. At that point, Miremba was vaguely familiar with climate change issues through school but never thought of her country's issues as part of the climate crisis. Days spent reading up on the subject, from scientific papers to

UN reports and activists' blogs, enabled her to start connecting the dots. She gained significant knowledge about the climate crisis; the cause–effect channels leading her country to witness such extreme weather, the factors behind the crisis, and the policies put forward to mitigate its impact theoretically. However, the more she read, the more concerned she got. Individuals around her were constantly talking about the heatwave and its devastating effects but never had they mentioned the connection to climate change. The most shocking part of it all was the knowledge gap. She could not comprehend how she only got to learn about this through her own research and so late in her life when the situation could only qualify as a global existential threat.

Progressively, she felt a responsibility to speak up and share her newly gained knowledge and began a quest for a relevant outlet. It was in that context that she first realised the power of the digital tools and platforms she grew up using. Enabling her to start her self-taught journey into learning about climate issues was only part of it. The other part was discovering and connecting with large communities of like-minded activists. She soon came across the story and work of the girl who was going to become the face of a new generation of environmental activists: Greta Thunberg. Her story as the sixteen-year-old girl who started a global movement of climate strikes and went on to confront global leaders and the highest political institutions around the world deeply inspired Miremba, as it inspired millions of others. Her digital engagement with this community cemented her beliefs in climate justice, intergenerational equity, fair green transitions and the need for systemic change.

Greta's story was also highly empowering. Her ability to transform her one-person strikes in front of the Swedish parliament into a highly vocal and visible global movement was proof that, as young as she was and as powerless as she felt, her generation had access to tools to make their voice heard, and she decided to do just that. By 2019, the Greta-inspired *Friday for Future Movement*, where young individuals skip school to go on strikes, had gained increasing exposure and participation worldwide, and Miremba decided to initiate it in Uganda. She started alone, in front of the parliament, armed with a homemade sign 'strike for the climate' and a smartphone connecting her to the online community of her peers. She knew awareness about climate change was even lower in her country and city and did not expect to be able to rally many voices as quickly as had happened in other countries, but she was still hopeful. Unfortunately, after twenty-four Friday strikes, a month and a half of protesting, she was still not able to convince a single person to join her despite the increasing popularity and excitement around the strikes in other parts of the world. Reasons for that ranged from fear of the police and authorities' reaction to protests to a lack of urgency to fatalistic inertia sentiments to different policy prioritisation. The standard narrative would usually be, 'How can we strike to protect the environment? There are so many issues we need to address first: corruption, poverty, famine, unemployment.'

While strongly identifying with the digital community of her peers in other countries, Miremba did feel significant differences. One reason was her inability to rally more voices to the cause in her country. Another was that she was not fighting a future threat or one with a minor impact on current daily lives; she was fighting something that had already turned the lives of whole communities around her upside down. She was outraged by the global unfairness inherent in the climate crisis. While being the least responsible for emissions, her continent is also the one suffering the most from them. So, she was seeking accountability and action from policymakers in her country and from policymakers worldwide. She firmly believed developed countries should be held accountable for the impact of their inaction outside of their own countries. The fact that voices from the African continent, developing countries, and 'the Global South' as she called it, were not getting as much attention and exposure was extremely frustrating.

However, she never felt like this was grounds to distance herself from the climate strikes movement. She was convinced that the climate crisis was the uniting cause. It was the only issue able to sustain convergence between various fights. So yes, she adhered to the intergenerational climate justice narrative, but she also believed climate was about justice for developing countries and justice for the most vulnerable populations in other counties and her own. Her fellow citizens' belief that fighting corruption, poverty and famine is a priority was to her an argument for, rather than against, climate activism because all these issues come together in the fight for climate justice. Gradually, her peers in developed countries started relaying the concerns specific to her country and continent. Over time, the movement started rallying other voices from the Global South. This digital community kept her going and fuelled her energy. In September 2019, when thousands of strikes were organised around the world with millions of participants, her voice finally started to be heard in the Global North and in her world. This led her to

Davos. She is here with other climate activists; they sleep in tents as another form of protest and are determined to confront world leaders and get their message out there at the one event that brings together the most influential individuals in the world. The most important day of their trip was 18 January. This was the day they were getting a seat at the table to talk with those in power.

Sitting in the communal tent, she tries to gather her thoughts and feelings after the round-table meeting. She knows they have been able to communicate their messages. They did not have one unique grievance, but she believes it is a strength since they can reflect the diversity of issues stemming from the climate crisis that converge into one single request: a request to act, act fast, act boldly and act now. The 'adults' in the room listened to them. They showed interest and concern. But she had mixed feelings. Speeches and talks which do not translate into any action have happened too many times for her to believe that this instance would be any different. However, at the end of the day, she thinks their power is not conditioned by these people but only by themselves. She knows that they *will* continue their fight, that they *can* continue their fight without the leaders, and that is an incredible achievement. Sooner or later, they will have to follow, she thought. As much as some like to portray them as powerless kids who do not comprehend the complexity of real-world issues, she knows that they have leverage; she knows there is hope. Growing the movement is the key. Miremba raised enough money from a crowdfunding campaign to start a green school and education initiative in Uganda.

PUBLIC POLICY AND CHANGE: THE MISSING LINK IS THE INDIVIDUAL

The stories of Tiberius, Camille, and Miremba could not seem more different, be it from a historical perspective, sociocultural contexts, public policy and institutional systems, or from the perspective of the characters themselves. Their beliefs are different, and so are their aspirations, their visions of life, their requests, their messages but also their ability to ask for change, their ability to enact change, their approach to doing so. However, the dynamics in these three stories can be boiled down to a set of common first principles, those same principles which should be at the heart of our analytical frameworks, the 'constants in the space–time continuum'.

Every social organisation, be it an empire, a country, a city, a neighbourhood or any other community, is motivated by a common goal. Public policies represent the rules and institutions that constrain or channel individual behaviour towards that common goal. On the receiving end of these public policies is a network of individuals motivated by their own interests, ambitions, beliefs, and also common values cemented by the community. As such, the interaction between the system of public policies and the network of individuals shapes the progress of social organisations towards their common goal. Where there is a convergence between the public policy system and the readiness of the network of individuals to absorb said public policies, individual and joint interests are aligned, and progress towards the common goal is accelerated and cohesive. Where there is divergence, speed of progress and cohesion is threatened. Our three stories are neither stories of systems nor individuals, but stories of interaction between the two. Moreover, they are first and foremost tales of divergence and imbalance. The divergence between the public policy system and the network of individuals on the receiving end of this system. The divergence between the Roman Republic, its institutions, its socio-economic policy choices, its narrative and the needs, beliefs and interests of the Roman people embodied by Tiberius and his supporters. Divergence between the French monarchy, its political legitimacy, its social order and the abilities, objectives and ambitions of the French people represented by the Assembly. Divergence between modern economic paradigms, profit-maximising narratives and the values of younger generations as illustrated by Miremba and her peers. It is a divergence that leads to the erosion of social cohesion apparent in protests, revolutions, civil war and social unrest.

As such, ignoring the network of individuals on the receiving end of public policies leads to a truncated vision of policy systems, unable to explain such events nor sustain resilient and efficient institutions. This is the main reason behind our initial paradox of progress vs inertia. Indeed, focusing our change analysis solely on public policy instruments leaves out a key constant of change in the space–time continuum: the individual. Bringing it back into the equation is fundamental to enabling the convergence needed to reconcile our operating frameworks in the context of structural transformations. In order to solve this challenge, we at Whiteshield have conducted a four-year-long multidisciplinary fundamental research project, collecting, analysing and exploiting more than 300 indicators and over a million data points related to both policy systems and networks of individuals including indicators of country development, public policy instruments, policy narratives, governance, trust and public legitimacy, social cohesion, community and sociological analysis, etc. Leveraging various statistical methodologies ranging from network to discourse analysis, we have generated a comprehensive development formula that aims to widen our narrow-sided traditional policy debates and guide more efficient, resilient and socially cohesive policy systems in a critical period of our civilisational history. This fundamental research enabled us to uncover critical development mechanisms with wide-ranging implications for the current state of the public policy world, from replacing the concept of GDP and other traditional development metrics with a Balance of Policy (BoP) to changing the traditional sectorial configuration of ministries. Our research points to the need to reform key aspects of public policy both in terms of policy analysis and conceptual frameworks but also policy practice and governance. Our book aims at introducing a new public policy code to help initiate this journey.

Chapter One

THE PUBLIC POLICY GAP

Public policy paradigms are not evolving at the same speed as development paradigms. We are trying to achieve new objectives and adapt to new contexts with outdated methodologies.

A MISALIGNMENT OF PARADIGMS

'Every problem of the world is a problem of thought', so said David Bohm, one of the founding fathers of quantum theory. If policymakers around the world are facing an impasse, it might be time to review our common frameworks and question assumptions that are taken for granted. The best timing to conduct such an exercise remains a crisis or a disruption. Indeed, crises offer a window of opportunity, a small time-bubble during which individuals are collectively drawn together to understand what went wrong and ask what it was that brought them here. The 2008 Financial Crisis came with its fair share of questions - experts and policymakers in the most powerful countries were humbled by their failure, a failure to understand the world's complexity and a deceptive feeling that they could control it. Beyond the first moments of panic, habits and business-as-usual took over. Perhaps the questions asked did not go far enough, or perhaps the exercise that started was just the premise, a premise to be revived by the next crisis. The next crisis came; it was deeper and new in nature. In the months and years that follow COVID-19, we must initiate a long overdue process of asking and reflecting on fundamental universal questions on what needs to be done to accelerate development and avoid the gloomiest scenarios.

We have entered a new development paradigm

Mission statements are one of those business concepts which have become a cliché while still holding significant legitimacy with experts, academia and businesses alike. Most of them are platitude-filled and awash with buzzwords and jargon. Every business will deem it necessary to have one, and every business professor will invite students to contemplate their importance. That is because the real-world quality of mission statements does not undermine the relevance and usefulness of the exercise, nor can we deny the power of a meaningful mission statement in unifying a social network around the firm.

We suggest engaging in a slightly different exercise: reflecting on the mission statement of societies. Not the vision of countries, not the agenda of policymakers, not the goals of governments but the actual purpose of societies as a meta-organisation of individuals. Some will argue that the question is by no means a new one; philosophers and social scientists have been raising it since the dawn of time.

Aristotle would argue that it promotes what he called 'flourishing lives'. Thomas Hobbes would say that social organisation is about trading some individual freedoms in exchange for safety and to avoid the inescapable state of war and conflict arising from natural human instinct. John Locke would point out the protection of natural rights. Jean-Jacques Rousseau would invoke the promotion of the common good and collective will be as defined by the majority.

Others will argue that it is a question that can only be explored in vain as any answer will be normative and cannot be generalised to a universal truth. This is partly true, but we can start by looking at our past and attempt to understand how, effectively, we have been answering this question for centuries. The first insight that History gives us is that defining development and the mission of societies is a continuously evolving task and a self-feeding one. What we consider today as development goals would not have been taken as such fifty years ago, and in fifty years, other development goals will also emerge. As economic structures change, as science and knowledge progress, and as social structures evolve, the frontier of what is achievable changes, and so does the list of challenges that societies need to address.

As such, one can see that throughout civilisation's history, we have periodically changed our development paradigms or how we commonly define a developed society.

To illustrate this point, we have identified a stylised four-development age framework. Each age includes a dominant societal direction (i.e. What are societies trying to achieve? What is their core mission?), a development paradigm, an economic paradigm and a set of features such as the frequency of disruptions, the management of resources and their surplus and the dominant voice of guidance in development (Figure 1).

The 1st age corresponds to the early days of societal organisations. The period is characterised by the transition from primitive forms of life to agricultural societies and early urban settlements. This formative stage of civilisation is based on a feeling of belonging to a group and subsequently operating in a way that benefits not only oneself but also the wider society. It relies on sharing and tradition (or social norms) to create order and social cohesion guided by a spiritual leader. Economically speaking, the key production factor is land, and the surplus of resources is shared within the community. The frequency of disruptions is low and mainly driven by external natural causes. The dominant societal direction is 'belonging' which means that the system is oriented towards maintaining a strong community, and development is centred around the well-being of said community.

The 2nd age is linked to the early days of nation building, military expansions and colonial empires. The trigger point which initiated a transition from the first to the 2nd age is the progressive monopolisation of the legitimate use of violence by a unique authority, the creation of the State. This leads to a concentration and centralisation of power. The development effectively amounts to military strength and the ability to expand the territory under control. The key production factor is labour, and the dominant economic paradigm revolves around more advanced agriculture, trade and early forms of industrialisation. The minority controls the surplus of resources in power, and the voice of guidance is the chancellor or the king's advisor. Cycles of disruption follow a medium frequency driven mainly by wars. The dominant societal direction is 'obeying' – the system is oriented towards maintaining order and control over people and resources.

Figure 1.   Evolution of development paradigms

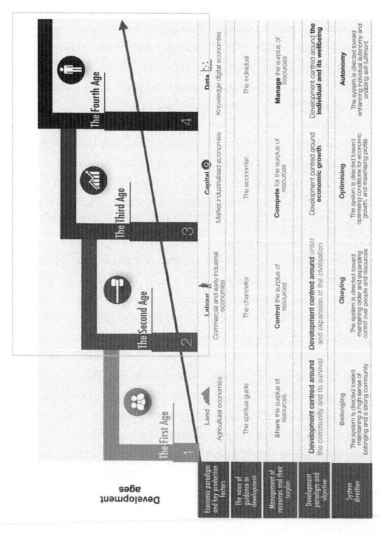

Development ages	The First Age 1	The Second Age 2	The Third Age 3	The Fourth Age 4
	Land	Labour	Capital	Data
Economic paradigm and key production factors	Agricultural economies	Commercial and early industrial economies	Market industrialised economies	Knowledge digital economies
The voice of guidance in development	The spiritual guide	The chancellor	The economist	The individual
Management of resources and their surplus	**Share** the surplus of resources	**Control** the surplus of resources	**Compete** for the surplus of resources	**Manage** the surplus of resources
Development paradigm and objective	Development centred around the community and its survival	Development centred around order and expansion of the civilisation	Development centred around economic growth	Development centred around the individual and its wellbeing
System direction	Belonging The system is directed toward maintaining a high sense of belonging and a strong community	Obeying The system is directed toward maintaining order and expanding control over people and resources	Optimising The system is directed toward optimising conditions for economic growth, and maximising profits	Autonomy The system is directed toward enhancing individual autonomy and enabling self-fulfilment

Source: Whiteshield

The 3rd age corresponds to modern nation-states. We situate the trigger point which initiated a progressive transition towards the 3rd age as the creation of the world's first stock exchange in Amsterdam. It is, however, the Industrial Revolution which will shape the key features of this 3rd age. Economically speaking, it is the age of industrialised market economies with capital as the dominant production factor and competition for the surplus of resources. The dominant development paradigm is one that prioritises economic growth and virtually equals the notion of development with economic performance. The voice of guidance in the development process is the economist. This age is characterised by high-frequency disruptions driven mainly by economic cycles. The dominant societal direction is 'optimising' which means that the civilisation system is oriented towards enhancing economic growth and competitiveness.

Finally, the 4th age describes our current societies. The main trigger point is digital technological disruption and its impact on our lives and socio-economic fabrics. The dominant economic paradigm is that of digital knowledge economies which revolve around data as the main production factor and are characterised by the importance of intangible assets, a type of 'capitalism without capital', and the rise of a new working model centred around collaborative networks and platforms.

We refer to the dominant societal direction in this 4th age as 'autonomy' because of the enhanced role of individuals in this civilisational system. The importance of individuals over time has been dependent on their proximity to power, knowledge and the tools of capital accumulation. Currently, as individuals we have more information, or data, at our fingertips than ever before. This may not sound like a fundamental change in the system; however, in many countries, it is acting as a mechanism for a rebalancing of power. Thanks to technology, but also societal changes such as the strengthening of post-materialist values, the autonomy of individuals is increasing, and their self-fulfilment is gaining as a priority among development goals. In this 4th age, the voice of guidance in the development process is the individual.

The enhanced autonomy of individuals implies the need for a citizen-centric approach to development centred around individual needs and well-being. The dominant development paradigm is no longer one that can afford to prioritise economic growth solely. Indeed, the turn of the millennium came with alternative development objectives and a questioning of traditional ones.

In 1998, Indian economist Amartya Sen was awarded the Nobel Prize in Economic Sciences for his work on human capabilities and his innovative approach to development, stating that it should be assessed via its actual impact on individuals' lives and understood as the continuous process of expanding their ability to 'be and do desirable things in life': being healthy, going to school or working. He paved the way for the notion of Human Development which came to life with the Human Development Index and the Multidimensional Poverty Index.

This initiated a general movement of finding alternative metrics to assess development and a proliferation of multidimensional indices attempting to encompass all aspects of development from economic to social and environmental dimensions. It also led to a reconsideration of subjective measures of well-being under the assumption that the role of development, the mission of societies, is to promote individual happiness or as Aristotle would say, 'flourishing lives'. The Gross National Happiness even became the constitutional goal of the country of Bhutan under the slogan of 'Gross National Happiness is more important than Gross National Product', pioneering a global movement that culminated in the adoption of the 2011 UN resolution 'Happiness: towards a holistic approach to development'. All this shaped where we stand today. Today, the Sustainable Development Agenda includes seventeen different goals recognised as different dimensions of development that societies should strive to achieve. This agenda represents a consensual understanding of development today, and it was officially adopted by 193 countries. And while criticism of the agenda did arise for several reasons, one cannot deny that it is unprecedented for 193 different societies to put on paper, explicitly, their mission statement.

Public policy paradigms need to catch up with development paradigms

So, we have witnessed the rise and fall of various development narratives (what societies strive to achieve) throughout history, and the same goes for public policy paradigms on what or who drives development (how societies can achieve their common goal).

From Philipp von Hörnigk, one of the founders of mercantilist theory in the 17th century, to Esther Duflo, winner of the Nobel Prize for Economic

Sciences for her work on alleviating poverty, and all development theories and theorists in between – including Adam Smith, David Hume, David Ricardo and post-Second World War development theories (the industrialisation school, the trade school, the structural transformation theories, the dependence theory, the Washington consensus, the goal-based approach and its pioneers Dani Rodrick and Joseph Stiglitz) – our conception and knowledge of what factors drive the material development and progress of countries have radically changed.

Similarly to the development paradigm, one can map the evolution of public policy paradigms throughout the history of civilisations. Four theoretical paradigms can be identified: Regal Powers, Policy Domains, Sectoral Policies and Citizen-centric Governance (Figure 2).

The first public policy paradigm is 'Regal Powers'; public policy analysis and knowledge of public policy were not yet systemic and codified. However, they still existed. The Hammurabian Code, written in the 18th century BC by the ruler of Babylon, represents one of the earliest recorded examples of conscious reflection on public policy, its aims and tools. The specific policies include a focus on order, law and justice.

Figure 2. Evolution of public policy paradigms

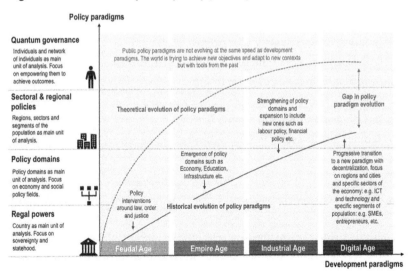

Source: Whiteshield

Moving to a more formalised public policy brings us into the age of 'Policy Domains', which puts empirical analysis at the forefront of public policy. Specific policy measures focus on the development stage ranging from business regulation and international trade through to gender equality and innovation.

The third paradigm of public policy, 'Sectoral Policies', moves away from the one-size-fits-all approach to one that recognises the complex nature of society by focusing specifically on components (sectors) of the economy or country. Political and economic geography are important aspects of policies and governance in this phase. A failure to recognise local needs or concerns can create disillusionment with policymakers and contribute to a breakdown in the trust or even the legitimacy of policymakers.

The final paradigm, 'Citizen-centric Governance', breaks away from policy-based silos and takes the individual as the main unit of analysis.

In an ideal scenario, as societies progress through the continuously evolving stages of development, public policy paradigms would follow as well. However, this has not been the reality.

A failure of public policy paradigms to keep up with development paradigms can help explain different political events during the last decade. The sentiment of disillusionment with policymakers is said to be one of the contributing forces behind the Trump victory in the 2016 US presidential election and the Brexit vote in the same year. Many parts of the United Kingdom were said to have felt ignored by policymakers in Westminster or Brussels. There was a substantial difference in the likelihood of Britons to vote to leave the European Union based on their socio-economic disadvantage and some regional aspects to the vote, although this tends to reflect the disadvantage. Those in London were some of the least likely to vote for Brexit, as were the Scottish. Both are geographically closest to the decision-making hearts of policy in the UK and Scotland.

Despite societal development progressing through the four stages, public policy has remained stuck in the Policy Domains and Sectorial Policies paradigms. Societies or countries have not achieved the optimal public policy paradigm adapted for their current level of development. There is a gap between the actual public policy paradigm and what is required – this is the public policy gap.

DIMINISHING RETURNS FROM PUBLIC POLICY

'The pace of change has never been this fast, yet it will never be this slow again.' these are the words spoken by Canadian Prime Minister Justin Trudeau in his opening speech at the World Economic Forum, Davos, in 2018. This sentence, which received a significant amount of attention, summarises a common narrative in the world: technology and scientific progress are increasing exponentially, change is everywhere and things are moving fast, perhaps too fast. However, we ought to be careful. This narrative can be misleading for several reasons. The subject matter here is change, not progress, not development, not growth: change. While it is undeniable that part of this change is positive, the overall direction the world is headed cannot be assumed to be as such, and by several metrics, it is simply not.

Indeed, exploring society or country performance trends for signs of a great acceleration remains vain. On the contrary, the dominant pattern is a deceleration or stagnation across the board of development metrics. Three main arguments can support this observation:

1. From a social perspective, we are facing potential social cohesion erosion and a decline in social capital.

2. By traditional economic metrics, the economic miracle is not fulfilling its promises.

3. Overwhelmingly, the world is not on track to achieve Sustainable Development Goals (SDGs), considered as an exhaustive and consensual definition of the desirable development path at present.

The world is facing trust erosion and a decline in social capital

Across the globe, we see a decline in interpersonal trust; that means how much we trust our fellow citizens. This reduction in interpersonal trust could have contributed to the fall in life satisfaction experienced in 2015. In the last decade, much of the developed world has seen a fall in trust and unstable levels of life satisfaction. Trust goes beyond trust in each other to include our trust in institutions, and both are important aspects of a fully functioning society. They are the basis of our connections and influence our actions.

A substantial part of today's corporate elite and policymakers favour the concentration of decision-making power. At face value, their rationale is often expressed in terms of higher efficiency and lower cost. However, by advocating for further consolidation, they implicitly assume that citizens and consumers must trust their abilities to maximise the well-being of the collective. Trust is a necessity in systems which are highly centralised; in these countries or political systems the government becomes the one point of failure. There is often a lack of citizen empowerment or engagement. Therefore, trust is needed to keep the system running (Figure 3). In contrast, in countries such as Switzerland or Denmark, the decentralised nature of decision-making means the need for trust is not a prerequisite as individuals are empowered to act; there are multiple actors responsible for resource allocation.

Falling levels of trust can be reflected by trends in voter turnout – since the 1980s, voter turnout among OECD members has reduced by over ten percentage points suggesting major reductions in social cohesion. Cross-country research has found that higher levels of societal and interpersonal trust are associated with higher voter turnout. Across the OECD, individuals tend to be more trusting of public service institutions than their national government. Less than 50% trust national government, whereas none of the four other public institutions fall below 50% (Figure 4). Low levels of trust in

Figure 3.   Path to reducing trust in government requirements

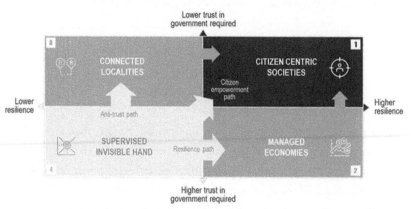

Source: Whiteshield & HBR

national government can lead to a range of challenges including an inability to enact policy change, to ensure micro-level behavioural changes (such as mask-wearing) and to instil public order.

These factors together could mean there has been a breakdown in the fabric of society and what bonds us together as citizens – hence, falling social capital. Indeed, in recent years there have been several large-scale movements which have aimed to bring about political, economic or social change. Between 2017 and 2020, there have been around 100 significant anti-government protests leading to the collapse of around 30 governments. In part due to social media and the ability of information to flow freely, these have not been isolated to local communities, countries or even continents – we have seen large-scale international calls for action. In recent times, we have Occupy Wall Street, which started in the US, the climate strikes, which started in Sweden, and Black Lives Matter, which again started in the US. All of these may have started in a specific city or country, but they have become globally known. There are other examples across the world where country-specific protests have gained traction due to data and information sharing, whether they are political uprisings in Belarus or the recent farming protests in India, which are being labelled the largest ever to occur.

Figure 4.   Evolution of voter turnout and trust in public sector – OECD countries

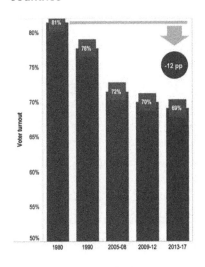
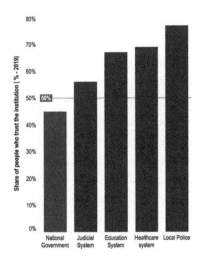

Source: Whiteshield, OECD

The technological miracle is not fulfilling its economic promises

If you think about your own daily life, you can find a lot of plausibility for the notion that things are speeding up. However, if you look at key economic indicators, things are not speeding up for one important measure: productivity growth.

In fact, by historical standards, productivity growth is pretty slow. Productivity growth has not stopped altogether, but since the mid-2000s, the rate of growth has fallen considerably. In Western Europe, the 1950s to the mid-1970s are often referred to as the golden era of economic growth – this is also reflected in its labour productivity. In the Euro Area, between 1950 and 1975 the average annual growth rate in labour productivity was 5% (Figure 5).

The annual growth rate of productivity has not been above 5% since 1976. In contrast, between 2013 and 2018 the annual productivity growth rate average was 1% (Figure 6).

Several hypotheses can be formulated to explain this productivity paradox. Some might argue that the most advanced countries (in terms of technological progress) are achieving higher labour productivity growth. However, the evidence allows us to refute this argument. For instance, the US has been averaging about 1.2% labour productivity growth per year since the mid-2000s compared to 3% per year in the mid-1990s. Suppose the slowdown after 2004 had not happened, and the US had kept going with the same average productivity growth from 1995 to 2004. That would mean GDP in 2017 would have been, conservatively speaking, US$3 trillion higher than it was. That is a loss of US$9200 in income per capita. Effectively, that means that Americans are poorer than they could have been. An issue that is certainly not helped by the decoupling of wages and productivity as a general trend in the world, where workers are capturing less and less of the already lower economic gains. The same trend can be witnessed in 29 out of the 30 OECD countries. Additionally, the opposite hypothesis, where emerging countries witness higher labour productivity growth due to a catching-up process also does not hold.

A common explanation given for this issue is the measurement problem: some experts state that we simply do not use the right metrics to accurately capture the economic gains from new technologies. That in itself is proof that traditional policy systems and their knowledge regime are not adapted to the 4th age of development. Using more appropriate metrics can help counter the glass-ceiling narrative in terms of economic gains from technology.

Figure 5.   Evolution of labour productivity annual growth rate in the Euro area

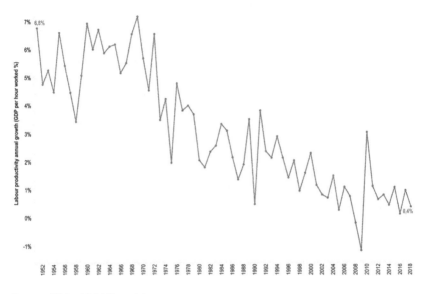

Source: Whiteshield, Eurostat

Figure 6.   Evolution of global labour productivity annual growth rate

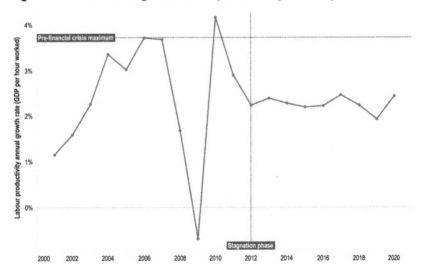

Source: Whiteshield, World Bank

However, the public policy world still relies on outdated and inadequate metrics such as GDP to guide decisions about a wide range of policy areas from public expenditure, to support of innovation and technology, etc. As such, the measurement issue actually contributes to diminishing returns from policy by misguiding policy decisions and consequently limiting the development potential to be derived from technological advancements.

The world is not on track to achieving SDGs

The Sustainable Development Agenda includes seventeen goals recognised as different dimensions of development that societies should strive to achieve. This agenda represents a consensual understanding of development. Consensual because, if nothing else, it was officially adopted by 193 countries. So, where do we stand today on SDGs? Are we on track to achieving them? The timeframe has been set for achieving SDGs with a deadline of 2030. Fifteen years to achieve a set of goals may seem like a long period of time, yet the scale of the challenge should not be underestimated. In 2019 and with only eleven years remaining to reach the goals, UN Deputy Secretary-General Amina Mohammed stated that '...we face a US$2.5 trillion annual SDG investment gap – a gap that is all the more acute in the world's most vulnerable countries and regions. At the current rate of investment, it will be impossible to achieve the SDGs by 2030. This is bad for individuals, bad for society, bad for the environment and bad for business.' The question is, therefore, what has happened in the last four years to get us into this position?

The lack of progress on SDGs is not limited to the most vulnerable countries and regions – it is seen across the spectrum of development and in all corners of the globe. To achieve the 17 goals, 169 targets were created, 21 of which matured in 2020. However, progress has been limited and, in some cases, there is insufficient evidence to provide an assessment of improvement. Of the 21 targets, only 3 had been achieved or were on target to be achieved by the end of 2020. Seven of the targets were deemed to be making no progress or even moving away from the target; if the 2020 picture is representative of the wider targets, then it seems impossible for the 2030 targets to be met.

The UN ranks countries based on their performance against the SDGs, the top ten countries are all highly developed nations within Europe, whereas the countries at the bottom of the ranking are less developed and in Africa. However, a rank of first does not necessarily equate to perfect performance. Sweden had the best performance on SDGs in 2020; however, it had achieved only four out of seventeen goals so far, was deemed to face challenges in nine goals and had significant to major challenges in four goals.

According to an analysis produced by the UN in 2020 there is not a single SDG where more than half of countries are expected to reach the goal by 2030 (Figure 7). Across all indicators, there is a significant amount of stagnation, suggesting countries may have hit the limit of what they can achieve.

The stagnation and failure to make progress on the goals is not a macro-level failure, and it impacts individual's lives. It is estimated that 3 billion individuals worldwide lack basic handwashing facilities at home, which is a core part of virus prevention and 1.6 billion workers in the informal economy risk losing their livelihoods. For too long, governments and businesses have preferred short-termism for which the cost has been reduced resilience and the lack of achievement of long-term goals, such as the SDGs.

Figure 7. Performance of the average country in SDGs

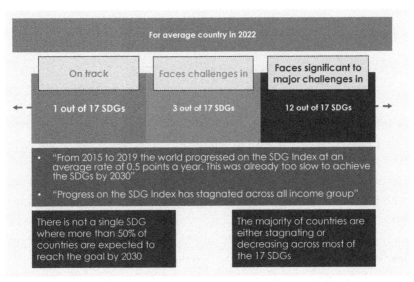

Note: on track - Responsible consumption and production; faces challenges:
Source: Whiteshield, UN SDG report 2020, 2022

Source: Whiteshield, UN data

As countries look to invest in alternative programmes with short-term benefits, there could be a reduction in the likelihood of the goals being achieved. Before COVID-19, the world was not on track to achieve the target to end poverty in all its forms by 2030; COVID-19 has created new challenges, including the first global increase in poverty in decades. Similar negative impacts of COVID-19 can be seen on other components of the SDGs, such as inclusive and equitable quality education, food security and the coverage of health programmes such as immunisation.

THE PRACTICE: REDUCTIONISM AND LINEARITY IN PUBLIC POLICY

The development glass ceiling and the misalignment between development and public policy paradigms reflect the need to shift towards the fourth policy stage, the Citizen-centric Governance paradigm. Conceptually, this shift would be hindered by two main factors.

The silo mindset obstructs the adoption of a holistic approach to development

While development objectives are integrated into nature and require a holistic approach, policy objectives and policy instruments alike are still framed within sectors, including but not limited to the economy, education, technology or the environment. This sectoral way of thinking is coupled with linearity assumptions: education policies drive education outcomes, market policies drive market outcomes, innovation policies drive innovation outcomes and so forth. The reality is much more complex: development goals are connected, trade-offs and synergies arise systematically, public interventions are not introduced in a vacuum, and their impact depends on and influences existing policies and outcomes across artificial sectors.

The issue of policy silos is not new; it has been repeatedly presented as a major constraint by several actors of public policy including international organisations such as the OECD, governments of different countries (such as the UK or Australia) as well as policy and public management scholars.

These scholars advocate for modes of governance more suitable to the complexity of policy challenges to break with the top-down, centralist approach of New Public Management, which further exacerbated the fragmentation of public services delivery. This rising concern has led to policymaking and public management practices such as whole-of-government approaches. Many emerged in the 1990s, such as the Delivery Unit in the UK, and are experiencing a resurgence of interest in the context of public sector reforms and complex policy problems – for instance in the Netherlands, Finland and France with its General Directorate for State Modernisation (DGME). However, it is predominantly argued that policy silos are persistent, and they are often used as an explanation for policy failures in the context of complex challenges such as climate change or inequalities. The position establishing the prevalence of policy silos can be biased due to the lack of indicators and measurements of coordination or collaboration mechanisms and policy integration.

Nevertheless, one might argue that this lack of monitoring is itself proof of a lack of policy integration: since these efforts are not monitored and rewarded, incentives to work effectively across silos are undermined. We argue that the prevalence of reductionist policy silos, despite acknowledgements of their induced challenges, is related to the perception of said silos as organisational and management issues in most cases. Indeed, most initiatives undertaken to mitigate the issue of policy silos are in the form of institutional mechanisms such as the creation of delivery units, time-bound, challenge-specific task forces or teams across ministerial portfolios. Even attempts to assess the degree of policy integration are often confined to assessing such institutional measures (e.g. the policy integration framework of the OECD).

However, it is precisely because practices such as whole-of-government approaches or national agendas are perceived to be exceptional tools that policy silos still represent the business-as-usual norm. Such institutional mechanisms are undermined by their inherent gap with the predominant reductionist paradigm of the policy world (whether it is in policy practice or research for policymaking). Breaking out of the silo approach requires more than institutional practices or mechanisms. Over time, society, technology and business has evolved. Whether it is through the invention of the light bulb or the movement to the open office, we have recognised the need to innovate to gain the most from the individual. However, the structure of our government has not changed to keep pace with the changes of society.

Indeed, it is fundamental to recognise that policy silos are not only related to the functioning of governments and administrations. Perhaps even more importantly, policy silos are also abstract constructions which shape the approach to policy challenges and the knowledge, analysis, formulation and implementation of policy interventions. The traditional approach of ministers, departments and silo-based policy agendas continues to reign supreme. however, just because something has always been does not mean it must continue, and we should consider alternatives (Figure 8).

A narrow vision of development confined to the policymaking realm

All policies are sociotechnical and happen in a sociotechnical system. Generalisation of their causal effect would require in-depth knowledge of all social and technical effects of the policy and of systems where it is implemented. However, not only is it difficult to have general rules explaining the

Figure 8.   Governance approach to reduce silos and enhance integration in policymaking

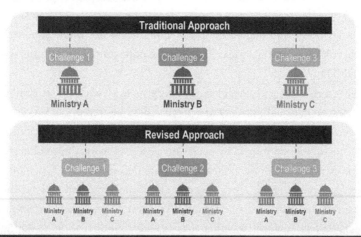

Source: Whiteshield

functioning of sociotechnical systems in the same way that anatomy explains the functioning of human bodies, *but also methods generally used to measure causality of policies fail to use insight* from relevant disciplines such as sociology, anthropology, psychology or even physics and mathematics. Secondly, the linear cause–effect paradigm exacerbates reductionism and the policy silo mindset. Focusing on proving the intended impact of a certain policy on an expected outcome through the current methods tends to downplay or ignore potential synergies with other policies from the same field or other fields, as well as trade-offs and adverse effects on other outcomes.

So, why do we need change?

It is clear that public policy paradigms have not kept pace with the stages of development. This may sound small or trivial, but it is not. Without policy decision-making and analysis matching the level of development, we will continue to see a disconnect between policy thinking and what is truly needed. The consequence of outdated thinking and macro-level analysis is an inability to progress beyond historical measurements of success, such as GDP. How can we achieve the Sustainable Development Goals if we do not alter our thinking, our measurement tools or our operations? We need change and the time is now.

Chapter Two

THE QUANTUM PRINCIPLE OF PUBLIC POLICY

$$D = E(P.L.A.N) \times Q(I.C)$$

A CHANGE OF UNIT AND QUANTUM GOVERNANCE

Having established that public policy is facing a gap materialised in a development glass ceiling, a misalignment with current development paradigms and practical challenges ranging from reductionism to linearity, our focus now turns to the solution: a change of unit.

Countless challenges and events justify this necessity, the most recent of which, in 2021, was the reality of a global pandemic. Every society wanted to limit the spread of the COVID-19 virus. It was an undeniable common goal. Among the most appraised public interventions to achieve that common goal was the introduction of social-distancing measures and the use of masks. Looking at which societies introduced these measures can help us understand part of the results and to what extent some countries have managed to contain the spread. However, it certainly does not give us the full picture. The full picture would require us to understand why in some countries these measures have been accepted by individuals, while in others they have been contested and dismissed. Individuals, or more specifically, networks of individuals are the key conversion factor that stands between public interventions and the achievement of common goals.

A closer look at the evolution of public policy paradigms shows that a key factor of change is the primary unit of analysis and the trend is the adoption of smaller and smaller units. Moving from Regal Powers to Policy Domains to Sectorial Policies, we indeed shifted from countries as the main unit to policy fields to specific regions or cities, sectors of the economy and segments of the population. However, we still have not managed to transition to the smallest unit of all: the individual, which would enable a holistic approach to development. Indeed, development goals are common aggregate objectives, and public policies are interventions at the society level. And for these interventions to lead to an aggregate outcome, they must first deliver an impact on individuals. The same is true when we think about business. Initially, a business that looks to engage in 'good' behaviour may consider donating to or supporting a charity. Then they broaden their activities to include corporate social responsibility and those who wish to go further focus on creating shared values between them, the government and their consumers. However, they fall short of the steps needed to have a true impact on individuals – external thought leadership.

In traditional mechanisms for change, individuals are grouped in abstract aggregates from public administration to the private sector to academia to civil society (Figure 9). But ultimately, every aggregate is nothing more than a network of individuals and the only vector of change is the impact on individual lives combined with the linkages effect or entanglement between them.

For far too long, our common reflection on development issues has been strained by the assumption that macro- and micro-level questions need to be addressed separately. There is a tendency in macro-level decision-making to strip individuals of their complexity and the full range of their attributes which is precisely what makes them unique.

Figure 9. Traditional approach to policymaking

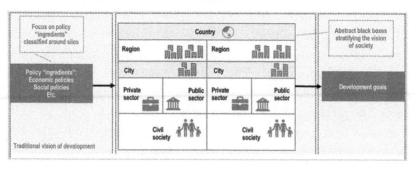

Source: Whiteshield

This leads to a portrayal of individuals as simple atomistic agents driven exclusively by the need to maximise their utility, the famous *homo economicus*. This simplistic approach significantly limits the ability to understand our societies and how they change and, from there, the quality of our interventions to accelerate the development process.

We argue that it is necessary to bring back individuals, in their full complexity, to change the formula.

A constant pattern in the evolution of development theories is the shift from understanding historical change to assessing policy interventions, leading the debate to focus on what public policies are critical for development: free and open markets, education and human capital policies; or innovation support, depending on prioritised development goals and on the state of our knowledge.

However, if we take a step back and reflect on the process of material progress in general, regardless of the specifics of development goals, *public policies* appear to be a critical factor of change, but cannot be the only one. Development goals are common aggregate objectives, and public policies are interventions at the society level. For these interventions to lead to an aggregate outcome, they must first deliver an impact on individuals. As such, and in order to bring back the individual into the development equation, we are introducing a citizen-centric policy framework. We call it Quantum Governance.

Quantum, because just as some of the most substantial discoveries of the century in natural sciences came from the study of the smallest units of the physical world in their full complexity, solving the biggest challenges of societies requires a similar approach by focusing on the most granular unit of the society: the individual. The behaviour of individuals is not linear or mechanistic as the Newtonian paradigm has suggested for centuries. What Einstein qualified as 'spooky action at distance' in reference to the ability of separated physical particles to share a condition and influence each other is perhaps one of the most obvious patterns of societies: influence through shared formal and informal institutions such as language, beliefs, values or myths. Human behaviour follows a quantum logic at the heart of which lies the concept of entanglement, leading us back to the idea that every social unit is a network of individuals and what matters is the absorption capacity of individuals and the strength of the network linkages. **Why governance**

and not government? When we think of government, it is a top-down system where policies or rules are created and passed down to citizens, and where decisions are made at the macro-level. This is not the optimal approach. Instead, Quantum Governance is a bottom-up system whereby the individual is the unit of measurement.

ENERGY AND QUANTUM LEARNING: THE FOUNDATIONS OF OUR DEVELOPMENT

The Quantum Governance framework relies on two main blocks: Energy and Quantum Learning.

Energy and quantum learning can be thought of as water and sponge or seed and soil. Energy is what policymakers put out into the world, just like a farmer may plant seeds. The desired outcome is not the sowing of seeds but the harvest of crops – similarly, it is not the aim of policymakers to create policies but to impact the lives of individuals. Once a seed has been sown, the chances of it successfully turning into a crop depend on the type of soil, the frequency with which it is watered and the existence of diseases or predators. Therefore, it is not just the act of sowing the seed that matters but the factors which affect the likelihood of success – this is Quantum Learning. An individual cannot successfully absorb a public policy if they do not have the right tools at their disposal to do so.

Firstly, The Energy block measures the overall energy introduced by aggregate-level interventions, including public policies and formal institutions. This block focuses on the drivers of development included in traditional paradigms with certain caveats: (1) emphasis on the policy 'mix' rather than policy 'ingredients' and (2) inclusion of policy energy multipliers such as policymaking narrative or administrative efficiency beyond the exclusive focus on technical instruments (Figure 10).

Secondly, the Quantum Learning block refers to the ability of individuals to absorb public interventions and act on them. The variables which shape this ability are the missing building blocks which should be at the heart of every change reflection. The importance of this absorption is not specific to the framework of public policies or even society development. It is a key lens of analysis for countless fields. In business administration,

Figure 10. Quantum principle of public policy

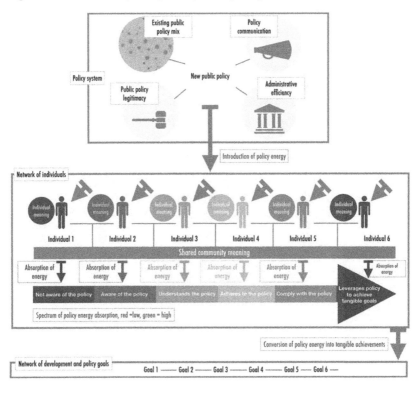

Source: Whiteshield

it is now common to talk about 'absorptive capacity' which refers to the ability to recognise the value of new information, assimilate it, and apply it for commercial ends. There are no grounds for confining this notion to the realm of business, innovation or even information (Figure 11). A firm introducing new management, incentives, or a training scheme should be aware of the absorptive capacity of employees and the capacity to convert the scheme into benefits and achievements. The same goes for a school, for a society, or for any type of organisation pursuing a specific set of goals.

This absorption capacity is constantly evolving throughout time but also across societies. Consider the example of loans. The earliest evidence of

Figure 11. Absorption of public policy energy by individuals

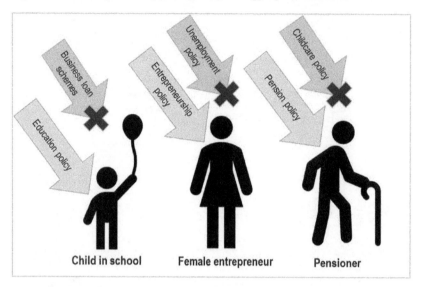

Child in school   Female entrepreneur   Pensioner

$$D = E(P.L.A.N) \times Q(I.C)$$

Source: Whiteshield

lending recorded in history dates back to around 2000 BC in the same region where the first human settlements were born: Mesopotamia. The full range of achievements that an individual can reach with a loan today, compared to 4000 years ago, is infinitely higher due to both individual-specific characteristics and the changing nature of social networks and linkages. And behind this expansion process lies the accumulation of human knowledge, experience and all its ramifications. Ultimately, the amplification of this absorption or conversion factor is the most powerful form of accumulated learning driving civilisational change.

THE QUANTUM EQUATION OF DEVELOPMENT

$$D = E(P.L.A.N) \times Q(I.C)$$

Building on this foundational framework, we introduce the *quantum equation of development* capturing Development Performance (D) as a function of Energy (E) and Quantum Learning (Q). The Energy input is itself a function of a country or society's policy mix (P), its legitimacy (L), its administrative efficiency (A) and its narrative (N) (Figure 12).

The Quantum Learning input is a function of individual meaning (I) which relates to the abilities, aspirations and motivations of individuals as conditioned by their background and their unique quality and community (C), which includes the core values, beliefs and norms common to the individuals of a community as part of the collective consciousness (Figure 13).

Overall, the equation can be considered as an equivalent to the production function for development and public policy. The Energy block represents the first input of the development function while the Quantum Learning block is the second input, and Development Performance is the output. This means that we can plot the development of each country as a function of one of the development inputs. For instance, in the case of the Energy block, the development function of a country returns the development performance for each level of energy, holding the quantum learning input constant. As such, each country would have a different development function depending on its quantum learning level. A useful metric to depict this is the Return on Energy (ROE), which is a ratio of the development performance and the level of energy invested. Two countries with the same level of energy will have a different ROE depending on their level of quantum learning (Figure 14). Additionally, the development function

Figure 12. Components of the Energy block

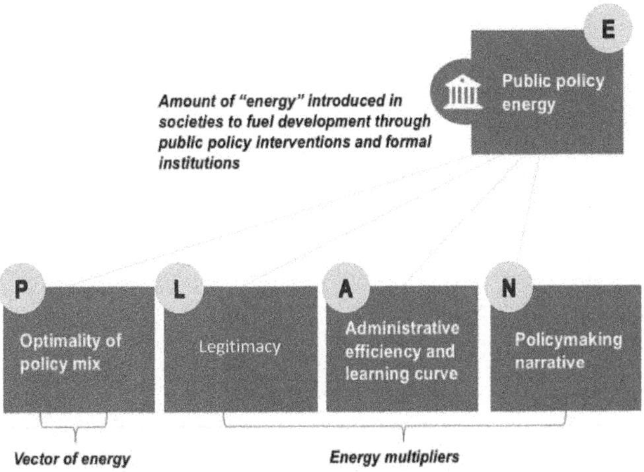

Source: Whiteshield

Figure 13. Components of the Quantum Learning block

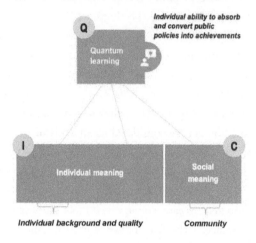

Source: Whiteshield

Figure 14. Graphical representation of the development function

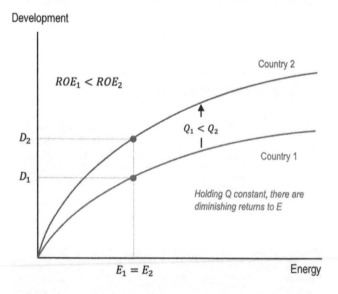

Source: Whiteshield

presents diminishing marginal returns which means, that holding everything else constant, an increase in energy inputs leads to a lower increase in incremental output. For the same country, the ROE decreases with higher energy levels if the quantum learning input is held constant. As such, one can speak of a development glass ceiling, where an exclusive focus on the Energy block leads to decreasing returns and increasing the ROE requires an increase in the quantum learning input.

The Duality of Society's Core Mission and Development Paths: Balance of Policy

In defining and redefining development, we need to distinguish between two broad types of missions or aspirations. There is the tangible side which includes the traditional development goals, for example, economic, technological, educational, social or environmental achievements. And then there is the intangible side, because as we introduce new policies, institutions, and techniques to achieve material development goals, the structure of societies changes as well, including all informal social institutions, norms, beliefs and relations.

While these changes happen, a mission that all societies should strive to achieve is strengthening trust because that bond is needed for the survival of societies.

The importance of trust or social cohesion is not a new theme and was at the heart of the new discipline of sociology in the 19th century and especially at the heart of French socialist, Émile Durkheim's work. Four centuries before that, Arab historian, philosopher and sociologist Ibn Khaldun in his cyclical theory on the rise and fall of civilisations, introduced the idea of 'asabiyya', which conceptually translates as social cohesion. He argued that its erosion is behind the decline and fall of civilisations later documented by Western historians.

The value of social cohesion is not exclusive to the collective level but also impacts individual outcomes, those at the heart of human development. A famous example of that is the well-documented 'Roseto effect'. Roseto is a town in eastern Pennsylvania, settled by immigrants from southern Italy in the 1880s. In the 1950s, the town began to gain attention when it was reported that deaths due to heart disease were dramatically lower than in neighbouring towns. Scientists could not explain it using the usual variables; the population did not have a healthy diet or lifestyle, and most of them worked in foundries. The answer to the mystery was in the informal institutions of this community, one that was distinguished by particularly high levels of trust, cooperation, solidarity and non-existent crime.

The duality between the tangible and intangible aspects of change should be carefully considered, and the paths chosen to achieve material development outcomes should take account of the impact on trust and cohesion. As such, a discussion of development cannot be conducted without consideration of social cohesion, and as our measurement metrics and analysis have focused on the material footprint of change and development, more investigation and measures of the immaterial side should be developed.

Ultimately, bringing change and development requires reconciling individual interests with common objectives, which is by no means an easy task to accomplish and requires carefully designed interventions. This aligns with Adam Smith's core writings on social change and institutions as opposed to the simplified understanding of his invisible hand in popular culture, the mantra of laissez-faire economics and neoclassical theories. To quote Adam Smith: 'in the great chessboard of human society, every single piece has a principle motion of its own, altogether different from that which the legislature might choose to impress upon it. If those two principles coincide and act in the same direction, the game of human society will go on easily and harmoniously. If they are opposite or different, the game will go on miserably, and the society must be at all times in the highest degree of disorder.'

The alignment between these two 'principles' as he calls them, cannot be taken for granted. It is not automatically fulfilled by self-interested individuals and stands at the heart of social cohesion or 'happy societies'. More specifically, cases where Quantum Learning or individual absorption increase faster than the policymaking Energy block, are not optimal for social cohesion maximisation. This is known as the individual pathway to development. In contrast, cases where Quantum Learning increases more slowly than the policymaking Energy block are not optimal for the speed of tangible development. This is the energy pathway to development. Striking the right balance between Quantum Learning and Energy is thus necessary to follow an accelerated and cohesive development path (Figure 15).

Figure 15. Development pathways depending on Energy and Quantum Learning blocks

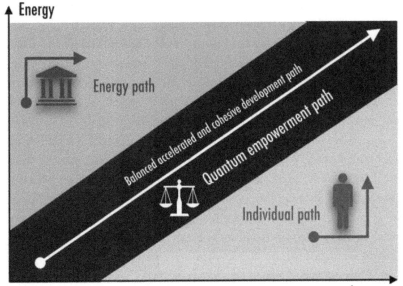

Source: Whiteshield

The Quantum Equation of Development in Practice

In order to illustrate our quantum equation of development and its validity, we engaged in modelling the current patterns of development for more than 151 countries.

Our first step was to identify a common development vision by which the performance of such a diversified set of countries could be assessed. Building on the findings of Chapter 1 and our framework of civilisational ages and development paradigms, we decided to adopt the Sustainable Development Agenda as our development 'north' in the modelling exercise. This choice was justified by the ratification of the agenda by 193 countries and the exhaustive list of policy goals included, which position the Sustainable Development Goals (SDGs) as a consensual and comprehensive definition of development in our current societies. As such, the Development block in our quantum equation of development 'D' was quantified via the performance of the countries included in the exercise in SDGs and, more specifically, in the measurable targets of each of the seventeen goals. The performance of each country was summarised via an SDG index following the methodology used by international organisations, including the United Nations.

The second step consisted of quantifying the Energy block and its four variables. In order to do so, we relied on a combination of fundamental proprietary research and secondary research depending on the variable in question. For instance, the optimality of the policy mix variable requires and extensive mathematical network analysis on a database combining time series of more than 300 policy instruments and policy goal indicators for 151 countries. We approached public policies and policy goals as a net-work, where each instrument or goal is a node connected to other nodes via linkages of influence and dependence. This allowed us to assess public pol-icy instruments while accounting for the various synergies and trade-offs which can arise between traditional policy sectors. In doing so, we man-aged to score each of our 151 countries on the optimality of their policy mix, where countries which are able to leverage these linkages by adopt-ing policies with the highest influence across the policy network score the highest. The administrative efficiency variable also required fundamental research based on complexity science tools. Assuming that the complexity of policy instruments implemented by a country is a reflection of the under-lying capabilities of its administrative system, we engaged in assessing the complexity of each policy instrument and, subsequently, the complexity of each policy system depending on the diversity and uniqueness of policies that it has in place. Finally, the legitimacy and the narrative variables were quantified using a combination of survey data, assessing variables such as trust in central governments, and social media discourse analysis, study-ing the alignment of country narratives with the development vision. As such, we were able to attribute a quantitative score for each country in the Energy block. Figure 16 plots the performance of each country in SDGs and in the Energy block.

The first fundamental finding is that despite the strong relationship between these two variables, we can still identify two key groups of countries: the first includes countries which are over-performing in SDGs given their Energy score, and the second includes countries which are under-performing given their Energy score. This is valid at all levels of development performance.

Figure 16. Performance of countries in SDGs compared to performance in Energy block

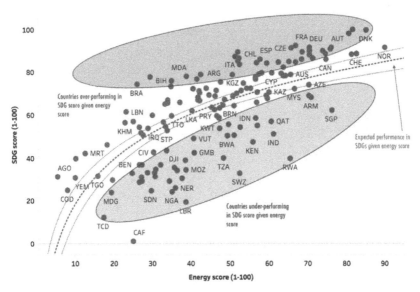

Source: Whiteshield

For instance, among high-development performers, France (FRA) presents an over-performance in SDGs compared to its Energy score, while Singapore (SGP) and the United Arab Emirates showcase an under-performance in SDGs given their Energy scores. Similarly, among middle- and low-development performers, a country such as Lebanon (LBN) over-performs in SDGs while Kuwait (KWT) under-performs given their respective Energy scores. This point justifies the assumption that policy systems, even when considering the variety of features that characterise them beyond the types of policy instruments they have in place, cannot alone account for development performance.

A second finding worth mentioning is the concave relationship between Energy and Development Performance which conveys the idea of a development glass ceiling (Figure 17). Holding everything else constant, the marginal returns on improvements in policy energy in terms of development gains are decreasing. Therefore, a sole focus on policy systems in development strategies cannot allow for an optimisation of development paths or progress rates.

These two main findings bring us to our third step: the quantification of quantum learning. Based on our foundational quantum principle of public

Figure 17. Decreasing marginal returns on Energy and the development glass ceiling

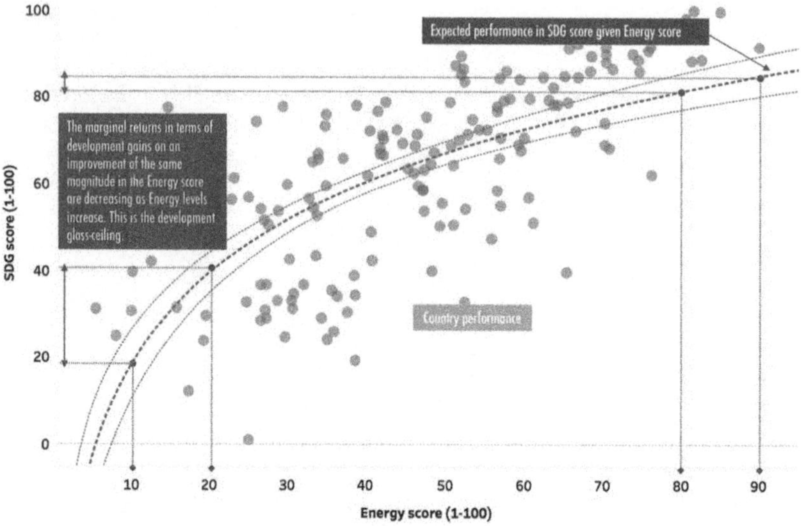

Source: Whiteshield

policy, we assume that every share of development performance that is not explained by policy systems can be explained by the gap between policy energy levels and the absorptive capacity of the network of individuals, or the quantum learning. We refer to this gap in the model as the 'quantum residual'. Therefore, the examples of countries showcasing an over-performance in SDGs (such as Lebanon), given their Energy block, are countries with a positive quantum residual, meaning a gap between energy and quantum learning in favour of quantum learning. Countries under-performing in SDGs compared to expected performance given the Energy score, such as the UAE, showcase a negative quantum residual, meaning a gap between energy and quantum learning in favour of energy. The approach used can be compared to the economic growth residual in the production function for the public-policy world. The identification of the quantum residual allows us to group countries included in our model into three categories as showcased in Figure 18.

The first group includes countries such as the United Arab Emirates and Singapore with a negative quantum residual; that is energy levels are higher than quantum learning. These countries are under-performing in SDGs given their Energy score due to a lag effect, whereby the lower absorptive capacity

Figure 18. Classification of countries according to the gap between Energy and Quantum Learning

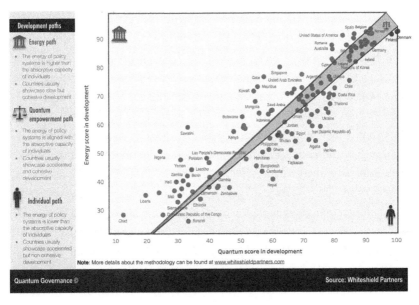

Source: Whiteshield

of the network of individuals slows the full conversion of policy energy into development gains.

The second group includes countries such as Gambia and Iceland with a quantum residual close to zero denoting a high balance between energy levels and quantum learning. These countries perform mostly as expected in SDGs given their Energy score because the alignment between the latter and the absorption capacity of individuals allows a reliable conversion of policy energy in development gains.

Finally, the third group includes countries such as Egypt and Thailand with a positive and high quantum residual, that is, countries where quantum learning is significantly higher than policy-energy levels. These countries are over-performing in SDGs since the high absorption capacity of individuals magnifies the conversion of policy energy into development goals.

Having illustrated in simplified terms how the quantum equation of development can be modelled in our current context, it is important to point to the implications of this exercise for the public policy world.

Firstly, it is fundamental to transition away from abstract policy domains and silos such as education policy, labour policy, and environmental policy. Our policy network exercise clearly highlights that linkages of influence and dependence between public policy instruments and policy goals transcend these abstract classifications, given the absence of a relationship between the strength of influence/dependence of policy instruments and goals, and the belonging to common traditional sectors. The implications for the public policy world of this first message are wide-ranging. Some are of an analytical nature, such as the need to develop new policy metrics that are able to account for these cross-sectorial linkages in order to better inform policy strategies and enhance policy integration and coherence. Others are of a practical nature, such as the required reforms in administrative systems, including the highest levels of governments, to transition away from the silo administration and enable a whole-of-government approach to become business-as-usual rather than a time-bound exceptional practice. And finally, some are both analytical and practical, such as the need to reform the education of public policy and training of future policymakers to go beyond the over-specialisation of knowledge in public policy, which relies on the reductionist paradigm of sectorial classifications.

Secondly, the public policy world needs to broaden its perspectives on its own subject (i.e. policy systems), and more specifically, to transition away from the sole focus on technical instruments of public policy, given that a wide range of other variables makes up the core of policy systems. Usually, a significant share of these variables is not accounted for given their intangible nature, be it the inherent capabilities of administrative systems, the strength of the legitimacy of the policy system, or the narratives introduced around development visions and policy mixes. Again, this brings up the need to revisit our traditional metrics in the public policy world and leverage new tools to measure these intangibles that we consider as energy multipliers and which should be prioritised as much as the tangible tools that we put in place.

Finally, policy systems are only part of the answer. The individuals, and more specifically their absorptive capacity, remain the key conversion factor. As mentioned previously, ignoring this conversion factor ultimately leads to a development glass ceiling, given that holding quantum learning constant, marginal returns on the energy of policy systems decrease. Additionally, measuring, accounting for, and leveraging this conversion factor in public-policy matters is now needed more than ever for two main reasons. The first reason relates to the public policy gap analysed in Chapter 1 and the development glass ceiling that we seem to be facing in both traditional development models, with a focus on economic metrics such as productivity, and relatively new ones such as the Sustainable Development Agenda.

The second reason links to our development age framework. As explained previously, the 4th age we are transitioning to is one where the societal direction and system are oriented towards enhancing individual autonomy. A combination of technological, socio-economic and cultural factors is empowering citizens and making them the core subject of development processes. The optimising age of focusing solely on growth, competitiveness and profits is fading away. Mobilising the same policy tools we used in this optimising age to solve the challenges and development issues of an era where the individual and individual well-being are the development 'north' cannot facilitate effective development strategies. In the age of enhanced decentralisation, where the individual, any individual, is empowered to become the voice of guidance in development processes, a citizen-centric framework which recognises the importance of this quantum learning variable and the ability of people to act as the key conversion factor is all the more relevant. This has several implications on public policy frameworks and practice.

The implications in terms of frameworks can be summarised by the expression new 'knowledge regime' or new 'code' for public policy. By that, we mean a new cognitive infrastructure to guide and support policy strategies. Part of this new infrastructure would include key policy metrics. The public policy world is in dire need of reviewing its traditional metrics. Gross domestic product (GDP) is obviously one such metric. The weaknesses of this 'device', which has come to hold such an important position in our policy frameworks, have been highlighted for decades and are only confirmed by our model. This also holds for other prominent frameworks, such as the Balance of Payments (the main accounting framework in public policy). It is necessary to keep in mind two important aspects of these traditional metrics. The first is that quantitative tools and data-related methodologies are not neutral. They frame issues, and therefore policy strategies and outcomes, in a specific direction. If this is ignored these tools can, under the assumption of data objectivity and neutrality, lead to multiple biases and raise mere assumptions to the standard of absolute truths. The second is that in the grander scheme of public policy and development history, these cognitive devices have not been around for that long, and they were initially created in very specific contexts (for instance, GDP dates back to the 1930s and was conceived in an attempt to measure production capabilities in times of war). This helps relativise the importance that we give them and makes it conceivable to question the pedestal that they have stood on in our modern policy frameworks in order to convert criticism and calls to amend them from mere calls to actual change. In the context of transitioning towards the 4th age of development, where development paradigms revolve around the individual and individual well-being and where economic paradigms are increasingly centred around digital business models and intangible assets, it is high time to shift away from the prioritisation of economic metrics, as well the focus on the material, tangible aspects of our development – two features which characterise GDP and the Balance of Payments. It is also time to think about and adopt new metrics to measure individual capabilities and transition from a mindset of cost accounting to a perspective of valuing these capabilities as an actual asset. In order to initiate this process, we have put forward several potential tools and concepts, including the quantum learning concept but also other ones, such as the Balance of Policy which is presented in Chapter 5.

In terms of public policy strategies and actions, several implications of the quantum equation of development can be highlighted. The first is the need to centre strategies around the individual, a task where new frameworks and metrics will be very helpful, as will be the leveraging of new technologies. The idea of advanced customisation, depending on the diversity of individual needs and capabilities, should not only become acceptable but also strongly desirable in public policy. This applies for policy instruments themselves but also for other aspects such as policy narratives and the need to strive for stories to which a diversified network of individuals can relate. It also applies to administrative systems and governance practices. We mentioned before the need to reform the 'horizontal' organisation of most public administrations around silos in order to fully account for and leverage linkages between traditional policy sectors. This reform is also needed to transition to a citizen-centric development and policy framework, given the intrinsic connectivity between these policy sectors in terms of individual lives and individual needs. In addition, this should be complemented by 'vertical' reforms in administrative systems in order to further enhance decentralisation and empower all levels of administrations to prioritise the citizen from high-level policy design and strategy to lower levels of service delivery. The implications of the quantum equation of development in the public policy world are tackled in depth in Chapter 5, which focuses on quantum governance as a practical application of our conceptual framework.

AN INTEMPORAL ANALYTICAL FRAMEWORK

Effectively, the quantum paradigm is a generic framework that can be applied to specific contexts by defining the development vision. In other words, development can be economic growth but also Sustainable Development Goals or Human Development or any other objective pursued by a society. This is precisely why the fundamental dynamics in our three introductory stories about Tiberius, Camille and Miremba can be boiled down to a common set of principles and analytical lenses despite the considerable differences in historical, sociocultural, economic and technological contexts. To illustrate this point, we will revisit our three stories through the lenses of the quantum development framework.

Tiberius, a 1st age Energy Block vs a 2nd Age Quantum Learning block

Energy Block

Focusing on the Energy block, meaning the interventions at the collective level, including public policies and formal institutions, the story of Tiberius depicts a policy system which fits into the 1st age of the development paradigm.

The **policy mix** is heavily oriented towards the organisation of the community and its protection against 'outsiders', as indicated by the prominence of regal powers and especially military and judiciary policy in the policy mix. This dual focus of the policy system is realised in the institutional set-up. Indeed, the Assemblies, one of the main institutions of the Roman Republic in charge of the legislative power, were comprised of two main bodies: *comitia tribute*, a civilian assembly in charge of domestic policy and the *comitia centuriata*, a military assembly in charge of war and foreign policy. In terms of domestic policy, the policy mix was mainly centred around what we could refer to in modern terms as judiciary policy, monetary policy and, to a lesser extent, tax policy. Taxation was relatively low and usually leveraged for military campaigns that were meant to provide a common good (i.e. the safety, security and independence of the community).

The legitimacy of the policy system is heavily tied to the community, given that the normative justifiability of laws and rules should be ensured by their contribution to the common good (functional legitimacy), popular sovereignty (affirmative legitimacy) and shared moral values (moral legitimacy) rather than individual authority of governors. This impersonal type of legitimacy where authority is linked to an office, a position shaped by rules and regulations rather than office holders, is the hallmark of the Roman Republic as a precursor to the modern state and the legal authority paradigm of German sociologist Max Weber's three types of legitimate rule.

The administration is still at a rather primitive stage, characteristic of the 1st age of development. It was intended for the governance of a small and homogeneous community. Indeed, the administrative system relies on the enrolment of young men from key leading families of the community and a high sense of civic pride and willingness to serve the Republic rather than a professionalised workforce.

Additionally, the administrative system featured an advanced system of checks and balances and this too was more suitable for a small community given that it involved a high share of informal rules rooted in moral values rather than legal norms, that it was guided by a principle of consensus rather than majority choice, and that it relied on public scrutiny as the ultimate accountability mechanism for administrators.

In the setting of our story, by mid-Republic, and as the community was extending in terms of population and geographical size, the complexity of the administrative system was already increasing significantly.

However, the additional layers of complexity were added to a base which was not designed for them. As such, several inefficiencies were arising of both a technical and ethical nature. The increasing need to assign administrators to far provinces, away from Roman public scrutiny, opened the door to more discretionary behaviour and subsequent issues of clientelism, corruption and inefficiencies.

The more complex challenges that the administrative system needed to face led to the mobilisation of private individuals in key tasks such as the collection of taxes by tax farmers, where private interest started to trump the common good, leading to oppression and extortion from tax farmers in the provinces. All in all, this meant that returns on administrative complexity were diminishing. The additional layers of complexity were not able to solve as many issues as they used to at the initial stages of the Republic, and more than that, they were creating new challenges and unintended consequences.

Finally, and following the dominant pattern here, the policy **narrative** is also heavily linked to the community, given that the four key themes shaping policy discourse are linked to the community. The first, *Libertas of the commonwealth*, revolves around the protection of the political independence and freedom of the community. The second, *Populus Romanus,* is linked to the importance of the sovereignty of the Roman people and the commonwealth, whose interests as a whole should trump those of any internal agent, be it a group or an individual. The third dominant theme was the glorification of Rome's founders and the *Patres* or Patricians. Patricians were allegedly the descendants of the first 100 men appointed as senators by Romulus, founder of Rome. These leading families had heroic exploits, high moral standards and values attributed to them and were portrayed as the ones who built the glory of Rome. The Roman citizen was thus systematically educated and conditioned to respect the authority of the Senate, to defer to nobility and to believe that the Roman state was in good hands when it was run by the descendants of those who had made it great. Finally, the fourth theme is the Roman values of *mos maiorum* which can be translated as 'ancestral custom',which represented the unwritten code of conduct of the Roman people. Roman values to be praised, respected and aspired too were essential in this code of conduct and represented a recurrent theme in the political and policy discourse.

Quantum Learning Block

Following this analysis of the Energy block, we need to review our second development block in order to fully understand the mechanics in place in Tiberius' story. That is the Quantum Learning block or the ability of individuals to absorb public interventions and convert them into tangible achievement. This ability is shaped by both individual and community meaning.

While the analysis of the Energy block in Tiberius' story showcased a policy system that generally fitted the 1st age of development, the Quantum

Learning block highlights a transition beyond this framework within individual and community meaning. The combination of demographic, economic, social and cultural transformations that the society in Tiberius' story was going through implies that the absorptive capacity of individuals was higher than the energy provided by the policy system.

Firstly, let us review in terms of **individual meaning,** which relates to the abilities, aspirations and motivations of individuals as conditioned by their background (economic, social and cultural capitals) and their unique quality. As mentioned previously, under the 1st age of development, the surplus of resources is shared across the community. This has several implications for the economic capital of individuals. The main one being the more or less homogeneous distribution of wealth. A second implication is the relatively limited impact of economic capital on the ability of individuals to absorb public interventions. Since the goal of these interventions under the 1st age of development is to benefit and protect the community as a whole, membership of the community rather than economic capital is what shapes the absorptive capacity of individuals. Several trends have initiated and accelerated a transition away from the 1st age of development in the economic capital of the Roman people under the Republic. Geographical expansion and military conquests brought a considerable amount of wealth into the Republic, which benefited only a small fraction of the population. There was a significant increase in economic capital inequality in the Roman Republic. In terms of economic mobility, while cases of upward mobility (as illustrated by the new nobles) existed, downward mobility was more common. Plebeians who were ejected from their lands, and could not find employment because of the substitution of freeman labour with slaves, saw their economic capital decrease significantly compared to their parents. All in all, these trends strengthened a transition towards the 2nd age of development, in terms of economic capital, where the surplus of resources is firmly controlled by a few people and where economic capital is a key variable shaping the potential achievements and absorption capacity of individuals.

In terms of social capital, a radical shift was occurring in the social fabric of the Roman Republic. Interactions between individuals from different social classes were decreasing. Indeed, the patronage system was losing traction. Patronage or *clientela* was the distinctive relationship between the patron and the client in Roman society whereby the patron was the protector, sponsor and benefactor of the client, typically of a lower social class or of lower wealth. These personal relationships enabled social stability and cohesion. However, by the 2nd century BC the practice was far less common for several reasons. These range from Plebeians greatly outnumbering patricians to greater reliance on slaves by wealthy people for all kinds of tasks and jobs which further limited interaction across socio-economic classes. Finally, new types of relationships based on individual loyalty and obedience rather than community allegiance started to emerge, especially in the army. Since the early soldiers were land-owning citizens, they did not have to rely on their general to give them a piece of land upon retirement. They did not require any retirement plans, because their farms and livelihood were waiting for them on their dismissal from service. This model worked well for a while, strongly legitimatised by a sense of belonging and ancestral Roman values. By mid-Republic however, the practice started shifting radically with a progressive diminution of the land-owning requirements of those joining the army, until it was removed all together by Gaius Marcus and reward schemes for soldiers from the generals were increased.

This is a fundamental evolution because soldiers relied on their generals to provide them with an opportunity to gain loot and with land upon retirement. The generals relied on their troops to give them complete loyalty and to support them in their goals to gain political power. The loyalty of the Roman legions started to shift away from the State in favour of the generals.

Finally, in the 1st age of development the cultural capital of individuals is relatively homogeneous and consists of the generational transmission of ancestral values and the beliefs of the community. In the early days of the Republic, the education of individuals followed a similar pattern. It was based on the *mos maiorum*, traditional Roman rules of conduct and was meant to teach a way of life, to shape characters rather than develop intellectual achievements. As Rome grew in size and in power, the importance of the family as the central unit within Roman society began to deteriorate, and with this decline, the old Roman system of education carried out by the paterfamilias deteriorated as well.

The cultural capital of individuals was witnessing an increasing differentiation depending on wealth and economic capital, and a rising importance of cultural capital in shaping individual achievements and access to the highest positions in society. In addition, there was a greater influence of Greek ideals and philosophy in cultural capital, especially for students reaching the level of rhetoric studies.

Secondly, let us review in terms of **community and social meaning**. If we had to depict a simplifying picture of what Roman social meaning was initially, this picture would include mainly legendary myths about Rome's History which shaped the majority of beliefs and values of the community. Indeed, early Roman history is shrouded in myth and legend. These myths, regardless of whether or not they were grounded in reality, are crucial because they reflected and nourished the social meaning, beliefs and actions of later Romans. As such, Romans had a strong respect for the past and were averse to change. Indeed, reformers had a difficult time passing their proposals and had to phrase their reforms as a return to something old, rather than as something new, in all periods of Roman history. Ancestral custom, which had made Rome great, had to be respected. Realistically, it is easy to assume that as long as the Republic was small, both in terms of population and geographical size, it benefitted from a strong social meaning fitting into the 1st age of development whereby a common language (Latin), a common ethnicity and a common religion united individuals. Their shared legendary past gave them a sense of purpose – that of serving the interests of the community, respecting and protecting ancestral Roman values, defending the Republic against foreigners and against anyone who was seeking to monopolise power, which could result in a restoration of the monarchy with all its issues.

As the Republic extended, the social meaning unsurprisingly started changing, becoming more complex due to new cultural influences and new demographic, social, economic and political realities. Expansion brought Rome into contact with many diverse cultures which meant a decrease in the homogeneity of the community and the social meaning. The most important of these foreign cultures was the Greek culture. This posed the question of how to deal with these outside cultures. Rome responded to this question with ambivalence: although Greek *doctrina* was attractive, it was also the culture of the defeated and enslaved. Indeed, much Greek culture was brought to Rome in the aftermath of military victories, as Roman soldiers returned home not only with works of art but also with Greeks who had been enslaved. Despite the ambivalence, nearly every facet of Roman culture was influenced by the Greeks. This cultural transformation meant a shift in the social meaning. Regardless of the official position on foreign cultures and influences, the reality was that new languages, new ethnicities, new religions and new cults were permeating the Roman community. The idea of a homogeneous commonwealth united by shared ancestors, language and religion, and also a shared past and values, was no longer a reality. The very definition of Roman identity was changing. Initially, many Romans, especially from the elite, viewed Roman identity as an immutable characteristic, something that they possessed by virtue of birth, rather than by virtue of attitude or activity. But as Rome expanded, Roman citizenship became an increasingly valuable commodity and the definition of what it meant to be 'Roman' shifted dramatically. Romans started advertising their inclusiveness and legitimatised it by the original myth of Romulus which was linked to the concept of a voluntary association of groups and individuals who came together on an equal footing to form a powerful whole. Ultimately, 'Romanness' came to be seen as both an attribute of civilised individuals and a tool of Roman expansionism while 'original' Romans still had a keen sense of their own exceptionalism. Ultimately, this led to competing definitions of the Roman identity.

By the late Republic, there were three distinct ways of understanding Roman citizenship: hereditary Romans understood Romanness to be a combination of ancestry and social and political participation; new men, such as Cicero, understood it to consist entirely of behaviour that conformed to Roman traditions of virtue and service to the state; and the new, Italian Romans saw it as a legal status to be acknowledged and enhanced by certain public behaviours. These shifts in the core definition of the Roman community were making it more and more difficult to sustain a social meaning which would perfectly fit the 1st age of development.

Camille and Robespierre, a 2nd Age Energy Block vs a 3rd Age Quantum Learning Block

Energy Block

The story of Robespierre and Camille depicts a policy system which fits in the 2nd age of development.

In terms of the **policy mix,** the common thread of public policies across the diversified domains of intervention was to ensure control (over people and resources), the authority of the system and maintain order and perennialism. Trade and industrial policy were means to orient the economy and resources in a desired direction, to assert the dominant social order and to increase political fidelity (through the granting of privileges). Tax policy was leveraged for military campaign purposes and to control resources rather than as a redistributive tool. The church and religious orders benefitted from financial immunities, and a large share of the nobles was exempted from taxation. Public policies on religion revolved around regulation of church actions, control of the authority of the Pope over French Catholics, abolition or consolidation of monastic orders, and regulation of relations with other religions and minorities. Cultural policy centred on protection, with authority over intellectuals through institutions such as l'Académie Française, as well as control of cultural outlets including books, newspapers, and theatrical productions through censorship.

In terms of **legitimacy,** the system follows the canvas of traditional legitimacy among Weber's pure types of legitimacy paradigms, whereby the right to exercise power is usually inherited and justified by the fact that it has existed for a long time. Indeed, we can clearly see this pattern of continuity in the legitimation of the French system at the time since it was inherent in the concept of a king itself: the king was held to have two bodies, a physical one, which necessarily decayed, and a spiritual one, which never died as highlighted by the famous acclamation 'le roi est mort, vive le roi!' (The king is dead, long live the king!). The system leveraged key justifications of authority to ensure an absolute exercise of power that could not be held accountable nor questioned by individuals or other institutions. These justifications included being a divine source of power, having a strong focus on tradition and the dynastic principle, family imagery portraying the authority of king as mirroring that of the head of the family, and ideological justification based on the Hobbesian school of thought.

In terms of **administration,** the system, despite the obstacles it encountered in doing so, strived to put in place a centralised command-and-control administration relying on officials answerable only to the leader of the control pyramid, the king. Louis XIV is the monarch who took the centralisation of government a step further and strengthened it. His council consisted of highly entrusted ministers outside of his circle of relatives. To carry out the decisions reached in his intimate and secret High Council, Louis relied chiefly on his provincial intendants. Stationed in the capital cities of France's thirty-odd généralités, or administrative districts, the intendants were, like the ministers, appointed by the king. In the généralités they could exercise the powers of police; raise military forces; regulate industrial, commercial, and agricultural matters; enforce censorship; administer the financial affairs of various communities; assign and collect taxes; and wield considerable judicial authority in civil and criminal affairs. These administrative reforms, intended to enhance centralised control in the context of increasing complexity, presented inherent contradictions with an administrative base characterised by a fragmented and territorial administrative structure with a patchwork of local privileges, historical differences and regional particularities. This led to recurrent inefficiencies which resulted in tensions such as the friction and hostility created by the intendants, or the inflexibility and the failure of reform attempts in several aspects of the administrative structure due to deeply entrenched vested interests (e.g. the failure to reform the tax administration and the tax-farming system). These inherent contradictions in the administrative system point to decreasing returns due to complexity.

Finally, in terms of **narrative,** its main objective was the glorification of the king and to nourish in the collective consciousness the need to answer to his authority without questioning it. Given the scarcity of instances of direct communication between the king and individuals and given that the narrative was at least partly shaped by those outside the closed boundaries of the court, a narrative-building process was progressively developed and came into place under Louis XIV. It combined ceremonies, rituals, symbolism and allegories, as well as art, architecture and the press as the main mediums to convey the narrative of the king's glorification and appraisal.

Quantum Learning block

While the analysis of the Energy block in Camille and Robespierre's story showcased a policy system that generally fits the 2nd age of development, the Quantum Learning block highlights a transition beyond this framework within the individual and community meaning.

Firstly, let us review in terms of **individual meaning.** An increasing gap was emerging between the socio-economic realities of the country and the antiquated hierarchy of social orde. Regarding economic capital, the rise of the bourgeoisie meant that the privileged orders no longer held a monopoly over the control of resources and their surplus. While industrial production was still at a relatively limited stage in the setting of our story, the rise of the bourgeoisie was already happening and strengthening, especially among the class of financiers, some liberal professions, and, in particular, large merchants and merchants-turned-producers. Indeed, most production continued to be centred in small artisanal workshops and power-driven machinery remained a rarity. The class that profited most from this situation in terms of economic capital was that of the merchants and merchants-turned-producers who led and shaped the growth in industry through organisational rather than technological changes. These changes included the development of a putting-out system through vast networks of local, regional and international markets and the connection of thousands of rural labourers in successive stages of production. They also included an increased division of labour in urban manufactories and a spatial concentration enabling economies of scale. The merchants managed to insert themselves between supply and demand, advancing raw materials or tools to producers and marketing the finished product. This class of high bourgeoisie managed to compete with the nobility in terms of economic capital accumulation and therefore to question the traditional social order. In parallel, the economic capital of several segments of the population was deteriorating including the peasantry, the provincial nobility and some segments of the urban population, such as small artisans and workmen.

In terms of social capital, a critical trend impacting individual meaning was the increasingly blurry lines between traditional social orders. The distinction between noble and commoner was not as clear as it used to be. Nobles were also involved in trade and finance, whilst many wealthy individuals from the bourgeoisie purchased patents of nobility. Rich commoners bought and married their way to social mobility. The bourgeoisie was also able to buy administrative and judicial offices, a practice which became quite common to resorb part of the state deficit and finance military campaigns. At the other end of the economic spectrum, boundaries also began to blur between the poor nobility and the peasants. The misery of the country noblemen was particularly great in areas where agriculture did not prove remunerative and where they were hardly better off than the farmers themselves. As such, and linked to the above, solidarity between members of the same order was also decreasing, especially within privileged orders. Indeed, a progressive divergence in the living conditions and interests of different segments of the two first social orders, the nobility and the clergy, implied a dilution of social relations and social solidarity within these orders. In the case of the nobility, it no longer constituted a social class with a consciousness of collective interests. They formed an incoherent mass of privileged persons, who were concerned primarily about their family interests. The petty provincial nobility detested the court nobility more than it did the Third Estate itself. A similar pattern can be noticed between the high and the low clergy. The low clergy did not participate in any way in the administration of their class.

By the end of the *ancien régime*, the low clergy showed itself increasingly hostile to the high clergy and increasingly close to the Third Estate.

Regarding cultural capital, access to education was on the rise, especially after the royal ordinances passed in 1698 and 1724 ordering each community to provide itself with a teacher. Education benefitted from a context of religious concurrence whereby different religious orders took it upon themselves to open primary and secondary schools in order to nourish the faith or convert children from an early age. By the end of the 18th century, religious influence on secondary schools started to weaken significantly, especially after the ban on the Jesuits and the rise of the Jansenist schools which were more liberal and rationalist in their instruction. Secondary schools progressively enabled a mixing of the elite, with rich nobles and bourgeoisie, as they became a prerequisite for an advanced, prestigious and honourable career. Oftentimes, the bourgeoisie had received a higher education, which they needed more than the nobles who were able to secure high state offices without merit or expertise.

Secondly, let us review in terms of **the community and the social meaning**. In the setting of Camille and Robespierre's story, structural tangible changes were impacting the social meaning of the community. Firstly, economic changes related to commercial developments and the rise of a class of high and middle bourgeoisie developing, in several cases, economic, social and cultural capitals exceeding those of the privileged orders. These socio-economic changes did not automatically create new values and beliefs, but they made it thinkable to develop meritocratic values, to question privileges by birth. They contributed to the breakdown of the system of social classification and opened the door for a shift towards an individualistic social fabric. Secondly, comes the matter of progressive territorial homogenisation and connectedness. France as a territory was becoming an increasingly cohesive space as opposed to a fragmented collection of provinces. This structural transformation was driven by a wide range of factors ranging from the development of transport infrastructure to the gradual homogenisation of administrative norms, the centralisation of key policies and administrative structures, enhanced mobility of workers (especially seasonal workers), and the development and promotion of printing and the press, including the *Gazette de France*. These various factors contributed to an enhanced territorial cohesion which in turn helped shape a national consciousness. Evidently, the construction of a national identity cannot be reduced to a matter of bricks and mortar, but these various tangible changes contributed to creating a single public sphere of discussion out of which it became possible to imagine a single national and public opinion.

A second type of transformation affecting the social meaning of the community in our story consisted of intangible political and cultural changes. In terms of language as a key driver of community, the most significant shift was the progressive expansion of the French language. The share of the population in the provinces who still used exclusively local languages was not insignificant, but a higher adoption of French was driven by several factors including the efforts of the monarchy. Although these efforts were not aimed at uniting the community via a common language, at least not as a conscious policy choice, they did lead to that impact once implemented and this also made a national identity conceivable. In addition to the linguistic factor, it is particularly important to mention the interaction between religion, ethnicity and political culture in the shaping of the French identity and particularly in the transition towards the notion of a civic representation of the collective community. Religion, as a common bond, eclipsed narratives around ethnicity and race, as well as local and regional identities. Between the 16th and 18th centuries, the clergy engaged in massive efforts to instruct and reform the peasantry and replace traditional superstitions with orthodox beliefs. Although these efforts did not aim at instilling a national identity, they did progressively erase much of the local and regional diversity by imposing what represented a uniform Catholic culture. Leveraging this and going further, the absolutist monarchic order, starting in the 17th century, carefully crafted a top-down national identity centred around the king with a divine order. The crown actively promoted the cult of the *patrie*, but it is important to differentiate it from the concept of nation, as the patriotism that the monarchy put forward was one which identified wholly with the persona of the King. In doing so, the monarchy managed to create a basis for a unified national community while deliberately keeping it divorced from any notion of a specifically French community that could compete with the King. However, this opened the door to a civic representation of the national community, one that was not linked to any ethnic considerations but was united by a common political culture embodied by the absolute monarchy. Counterintuitively, this paved the way, at least partly, for the national 'awakening' of the 1789 revolution in the sense that the calls to revive French patriotism followed a similarly civic perspective, not attempting any return to an ethnic representation or invocation of the land and its cultural specificity but only replacing obedience to the King as the cement of this civic community by the collective sovereignty of the people.

Finally, in attempting to understand the social meaning of this civic collective community, it is necessary to remind ourselves of the influence of the Age of Enlightenment. While the thinkers commonly grouped among the Enlightenment philosophers differed quite significantly from an epistemological perspective, a series of common themes that will be heavily picked up by the leaders of the Revolution can be highlighted. For instance, the sharp criticism of absolutism showcased in Voltaire's work, in Montesquieu's defence of mixed governments and separation of power, or in Jean-Jacques Rousseau's theory of the social contract. Since men are by nature free, Rousseau argued, the only natural and legitimate polity is one in which all members are citizens with equal rights and have the ability to participate in making the laws under which they live thus presenting popular sovereignty as the ultimate source of political legitimacy. Another common theme is the defence of individual liberties as well as the criticism of religious orthodoxy. These ideological shifts were in some ways limited to a narrow segment of society, mostly to educated high and middle bourgeoisie, and a low share of the privileged orders who defended these ideals despite them being antagonistic to their privileges and their legitimacy. However, the Enlightenment ideals unquestionably represented a fertile framework for the leaders of the Revolution who worked to spread them and further contextualised them through speeches, pamphlets and newspapers.

Miremba, a 3rd age Energy block vs a 4th age Quantum Learning block

Before tackling Miremba's story analysis, it is important to mention that it allows us to highlight an important message about the unit of analysis. So far, we have focused the conceptual presentation of the quantum development paradigm around the national unit, given that it remains the dominant one in the policymaking realm. However, our aim is to introduce a framework that is valid not only for other levels – infranational and supranational – but also other types of social organisation beyond the political sphere (i.e. firms, schools, associations, etc). In the case of Miremba's story, the spontaneous choice is that of a global unit, given that we are dealing with a global movement. As such, we will focus the analysis of Miremba's story on the dominant paradigm across countries for both the Energy and the Quantum Learning blocks, rather than a country-specific analysis. That in itself should be considered as a first learning from Miremba's illustrative story, which is the necessity to take into account the rising importance of other units of analysis in the public policy world and the necessity to part ways with a methodological nationalism when relevant.

Energy block

Compared to other policy systems presented in our stories, the dominant paradigm in Miremba's story is obviously the closest to our current system and has witnessed several structural transformations to get there. However, we will focus mainly on the analysis of characteristics that make it fit into the 3rd age of development.

In terms of the **policy mix**, this is reflected in a convergence of public policies, in its various fields, towards the optimisation of conditions for economic growth. Obviously, the diversity of fields or domains included in policy mixes has increased significantly, expanding to fields where public interventions were non-existent to inconceivable decades ago. However, an important observation is how the majority of interventions in various policy fields are linked to the optimisation objective, optimisation of economic outcomes. Countless examples can be given, such as the orientation of education policies towards the narrative of investment in human capital as a driver of growth in a knowledge economy, the leveraging of environmental policies as a motor of economic growth via the opportunities of the green economy, or administrative reforms as a driver of foreign investment attractiveness. The orientation of the policy mix towards the optimising paradigm is also conveyed by the increasingly technical focus of public policies around the ideal of 'what matters is what works', the over-specialisation of knowledge for public policy and the dominance of economics and economic reasoning in the knowledge regime of policy mixes.

In terms of **legitimacy**, a major feature which follows the optic of the 'optimising' paradigm is the enhanced importance gained by an instrumental conception of legitimation that is 'performance legitimacy'. This model entails reliance on accomplishment of concrete goals, such as economic growth and job creation, and the ability and expertise to do so as a basis for rising legitimacy. This is partly linked to evidence-based policymaking and the spirit of 'what matters is what works'. When effectiveness is the paramount criteria to judge public policies, then the ability to choose and implement policies that work becomes a significant source of legitimacy for the policymaker. The reason this fits particularly well into the 'optimising' paradigm is that it provides incentives for policymakers to optimize, claim to optimise, or claim the ability and expertise to optimise, in order to gain further legitimacy. Legitimacy by performance obviously raises the question of 'performance in what?' And here the dominant pattern is performance in an economy-related objective be it GDP growth, job creation, international trade balance or fiscal balance. Obviously, this remains a stylised account of the dominant paradigm – other policy goals have risen in priority depending on the country and should thus be included in the performance criteria of legitimacy. Technocratic ideals have been criticised extensively, and admittedly expertise and performance are not sufficient conditions for legitimacy in several countries but the objective is to provide a picture of the dominant framework and showcase how it fits into the 'optimising' logic.

In terms of the **administrative system**, here again features of a dominant paradigm that follows the 'optimising' logic can be clearly highlighted. A core driver of that is the 'New Public Management' movement as a dominant public administration ideal since the 1980s. The movement is structured around new practices, organisational and process-related, and mainly driven by cost-containment purposes but also aimed at injecting principles of competition, strategic leadership and performance management from the private sector in attempts to enhance the efficiency of the administrative system. It has had several effects on administrative systems of which two are particularly worth mentioning. Firstly, there is over-specialisation and a silo mindset. The public sector management systems that were created over the last decades under New Public Management concentrated on precision-target systems, focusing on the performance of programmes or agencies on the 'frog view', rather than on the cross-organisation outcome level. Thus, the effects of interventions were analysed within their specific domains, or policy silos, while the broader interdependencies and outcomes received little attention.

Secondly, there is the audit culture and alienation of targets. With the development of these advanced performance monitoring systems, targets are often imposed from above to local actors. They are usually disconnected from the daily work of these local operators or the experience of beneficiaries. This can lead to an 'audit culture' where targets and metrics are alienated from real experience by a 'box-ticking mentality where as long as the target is achieved, the impact on the patient, student, etc. is secondary'.

Finally, dominant **narratives**, although transitioning to advertise goals beyond economic goals still reflect features of the optimisation paradigm. In the case of climate change and sustainability, the theme of our story, dominant narratives tend to focus on tales of a win-win scenario combining economic and environmental gains through a focus on technology and efficiency where economic gains and positive environmental impact can go hand-in-hand, thanks to green growth.

Quantum Learning block

Our analysis of the Energy block highlighted that the dominating policy system at play in Miremba's story shares strong features of the 3rd age of development. The analysis of the Quantum Learning block, on the other hand, shows early signs of a transition towards the 4th age.

Firstly, in terms of **individual meaning**, we will focus on a particular point with great importance in Miremba's story. That is the impact of technology on an individual's quantum learning via its interaction with the three capitals. More specifically, what we can see in Miremba's story is how the technology of the digital age can expand the initial stock of the three capitals for individuals and thus enhance individual autonomy.

In terms of economic capital, Miremba's experience highlights one of the channels through which digital technologies can help expand the individual's initial economic capital and from there expand the realm of potential personal objectives achievable. The channel in this case is peer-to-peer crowd-funding but the same could apply for other mechanisms, be it the ability to work as self-employed and sell services across the globe, starting a digital business, leveraging the economic opportunities of the digital economy in a business venture, or expanding the range of physical markets for an existing business.

In terms of social capital, the role of technology in building and strengthening a personal network is rather obvious at this stage and is further highlighted in our story through the experience of Greta Thunberg who managed to transition from a one-person movement to a digital network of millions of individuals, ultimately translating into a physical movement of the same size. Similarly, Miremba's weak initial social capital has been compensated for by the large community of digital connections that she was able to build and leverage for her cause.

Finally, in terms of cultural capital, here again the impact highlighted in the story is rather straightforward given that the key characters were able to access a vast amount of educational resources, and to connect with communities of experts and become highly knowledgeable. The impact was far greater than it would have been had they relied exclusively on traditional sources of cultural capital in their subjects of interest (i.e. climate change and sustainability).

It is important to recall here that our story remains a simplified, stylised picture of a far more complex reality. The interaction of technology with individual meaning and its impact on the stock of the three capitals is a fundamental question and the answer is not straightforward. Several factors should be taken into account, be it the differentiated impact depending on the initial stock of the three capitals, or inequalities of access to technology, skills and abilities required to leverage technology as a multiplier of individual capitals. It is particularly important to note that the impact of technology on individual meaning depends on the initial stock of the capitals and this relationship is certainly not a linear one.

This relationship can be conceptualised, again in stylised terms, around four main categories of individuals. Firstly, there are individuals with a minimum initial stock of capitals who actually suffer from a disempowerment due to technological disruptions. Excluded from the technological ecosystem, they risk suffering from a decrease of their initial stock of capitals due to a displacement effect. This means that the importance of technology is so high for individual achievements, that their exclusion from this ecosystem inherently reduces the realm of accomplishments at which they could have aimed. Secondly, there are individuals with a low to medium-low stock of initial capitals, with a low probability of seeing their individual meaning impacted by technology. These would include, for instance, individuals who interact with technological tools but do not have skills advanced enough to actually leverage them. Thirdly, there are individuals with a medium to high initial stock of capitals. These are the best positioned to enjoy a high magnifying impact from technology on their initial stock of capitals. Finally, there are individuals with a high to maximum initial stock of capitals. They are positioned to enjoy a positive magnifying impact from technological tools, but their initial stock of capitals is so high that the marginal impact of technology remains lower than for individuals of the third category.

Secondly, in terms of **community and social meaning**, collective structural changes are enabling a critical distancing from the mainstream 'optimisation' paradigm through the strengthening of post-materialist values, and the 'desacralisation' of core beliefs and stakeholders associated with the 'optimisation' framework. The theory of post-materialist values was first presented by American political scientist Ronald Inglehart in the 1970s, stating that as survival in terms of political and economic stability and prosperity becomes taken for granted, individuals and communities would start prioritising non-materialist goals and values such as self-expression, autonomy, environmental protection, freedom of speech, and gender equality over materialist values such as economic growth. Inglehart posited that as new generational cohorts would experience growing up in safe and prosperous socio- economic environments, communities would witness a general shift towards post-materialist values. Although empirical evidence of the theory remains mixed and even if, theoretically, this would only be valid for individuals in developed countries, it is becoming commonly admitted that more recently born age cohorts do indeed tend to emphasise post-materialist values much more with potentially a universal reach given the magnifying impact of technology and social media. This remains part of a broader process of post-modernism which generally revokes norms limiting individual self-expression including, for instance, bureaucratic and hierarchical paradigms. The strengthening of post-materialist values and the desacralisation of the optimisation paradigm is also accelerated by economic crisis. The 2008 Financial Crisis, in particular, became a critical event in collective memories, a constant reminder of the fallacies of economic doctrines raised to the standard of universal truths. In the wake of the 2008 Financial Crisis, the US Federal Reserve Chair, Alan Greenspan, famously declared: 'I made a mistake in presuming that the self-interests of organisations, specifically banks and others, were such that they were best capable of protecting their own shareholders and their equity in the firms.' The mistake he was referring to was not an individual one, but one shared universally, that came to prove markets were not immune to inefficiencies and mistakes, a lesson relayed time and time again since then not only by international organisations, experts, and school curriculums but also by individual experiences. Its impact on the collective consciousness should not be undermined, especially for generations whose first experience in the economy would coincide with a breakdown of the system and a slow recovery, thus changing the image that they hold of corporations, banks, financial institutions and the economic system in general.

Additionally, technological disruptions and the emergence and strengthening of new business paradigms in the digital economy led to a new business culture that emphasised the focus on networks, collaboration, creativity, agility and became a major disrupter of 'old-school' corporate culture, replacing the myth of the diligent worker slowly climbing the corporate ladder by that of the successful entrepreneur starting a business venture from a garage. Obviously, incumbent corporations would end up adopting several aspects of this new business culture, and what were once small start-ups would grow up to massive corporations replicating a fair share of traditional business-as-usual norms. However, the impact on collective values and beliefs cannot be undermined including a growing disdain for classic corporate careers, a higher emphasis on individual autonomy and a changing relationship to work with aspirations to have purposeful careers more out of passion than necessity. The digital start-up might have evolved to become closer to classic corporations in terms of core mechanisms, but it has nonetheless contributed to worsening the image of the big corporation in collective minds, especially younger ones. The image of the 'evil corporation' has become a mainstream one in popular culture, fuelled by artistic productions, journalistic work, individual stories and the more attractive start-up culture. As much as a firm like Google is currently accused of flaws not different and even larger than those attributed to classic big corporations, it did start its journey with a motto of 'Don't be evil'.

Finally, the community and social meaning is also impacted by the diversification of societal and individual identities and identification processes. A combination of rising global risks, intensifying globalisation, technological disruptions and normative cultural shifts is enhancing the rise of cosmopolitanism both as a necessity and a valued normative system to aspire to. The result is the emergence of interacting processes of cosmopolitanism. A first process is a sociocognitive one and consists of being able to see new connections between things that were previously seen as separate producing shifts in the self-understanding of contemporary societies and in the way they imagine the world. This becomes a generative process through the creation of new ideas, new perceptions of problems, and new interpretations of meta-norms (liberty, freedom, autonomy, equality, etc.). This is the first step towards the emergence and strengthening of cosmopolitanism as a societal norm, ultimately leading to changes in consciousness, active societal mobilisation and finally institutionalisation.

The cosmopolitan imaginary is already part of nations today. There are few national identities that can exclude cosmopolitan challenges, be it the integration of minorities, human rights or the need for global dialogue. Homogeneous national identities have increasingly come under scrutiny in societies that are more conscious of their multi-ethnicity. There is considerable empirical evidence in many societies of increased multiple identities, especially among young people. The phenomenon of global protests and societal mobilisation is rapidly increasing, and Miremba's story is one illustration of this transformative process resulting from the cognitive shifts in the conceptualisation of global issues such as climate change. The institutionalisation aspect is also visible through the strengthening of international governance organisation and requests for action at the global level in the context of various challenges including climate change.

Five key messages from the stories of Tiberius, Camille and Robespierre, and Miremba To conclude our analysis of the three stories we will summarise the common lessons that we can derive from them along 5 key messages.

1. *What matters is the interaction between policy systems (Energy block) and absorption capacity of networks of individuals (Quantum Learning block)*

This represents the foundational component of our quantum governance framework and the most important message conveyed by our three stories. Had we followed a traditional approach to public policy in our analysis of the stories, our focus would have been restrained to policy outcomes, the public policies put in place and how they link to said outcomes. In other words, we would have focused on explaining the military success of Rome, its economic growth and its rising inequalities by considering mainly its military, economic and social policies. We would have focused on understanding 18th-century France's economic situation, public deficit and inequalities through its military, taxation and economic policies. Finally, we would have attempted to explain social, economic and environmental performance in the 21st century via the prism of the various domains of public policy: economic, educational, environmental, taxation, technology, etc. In all three cases, this analytical framework wouldn't have been enough to account for nor explain the main events taking place in our stories. In fact, had we constrained our attention to policy systems, we would have noticed several signs of adaptation and transition in those systems, be it the distribution of lands to lower-class Romans and the military reforms to allow them to enrol in the army in Tiberius' story, or the administrative, taxation and economic reforms introduced by the reformist ministers of Louis XVI in Camille and Robespierre's story, or the environmental policies and green growth strategies in Miremba's story. However, in all three cases these policy efforts were not enough to ensure a cohesive development, leading to social unrest outbursts which can only be explained by looking at the interaction between the policy system and the quantum learning.

At the heart of the three stories is a divergence between the Energy block or policy system and the Quantum Learning block or absorption capacity of the network of individuals (Figure 19). This divergence is the key driver of the events of social unrest based on a development path showcasing a gap between the Quantum Learning block and the Energy block.

In the case of Tiberius' story, the gap was between an Energy block which fits in the 1st age of development and a Quantum Learning block transitioning towards the second age. It is in this context that Tiberius decided to revive an old land reform setting a limit for public land that can be used by individuals and redistribute the land in excess to Romans who did not have any. This action triggered a wide range of consequences that would culminate, in the short term, in the assassination of Tiberius and, in the long term, would contribute to the fall of the Republic. The senators who vehemently opposed the land reform of Tiberius were self-proclaimed guardians of a policy system based on the 'belonging' spirit where every policy should seek not just majority support but full consensus. They justified their violent acts towards him by leveraging a foundational myth of social meaning, that when Brutus created the Roman Republic, he initiated an oath swearing to never again allow a King to rule. They portrayed Tiberius as a threat to the core values of the Republic, as someone who was seeking individual power and authority. But despite this, a significant number of Romans sided with Tiberius because the quantum learning was transitioning away from this 'belonging' spirit. A cognitive dissonance was emerging between the policy system defended by those senators and their own individual meaning given that their rising economic capital opened doors to the prioritisation of individual interests conflicting

Figure 19.   Summary of the quantum governance analysis in the three stories

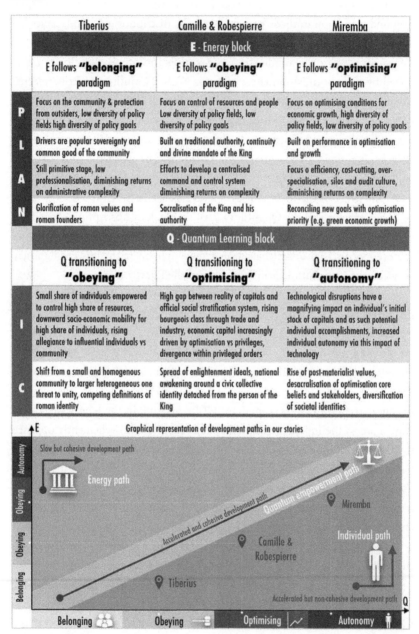

	Tiberius	Camille & Robespierre	Miremba
	E - Energy block		
	E follows **"belonging"** paradigm	E follows **"obeying"** paradigm	E follows **"optimising"** paradigm
P	Focus on the community & protection from outsiders, low diversity of policy fields high diversity of policy goals	Focus on control of resources and people Low diversity of policy fields, low diversity of policy goals	Focus on optimising conditions for economic growth, high diversity of policy fields, low diversity of policy goals
L	Drivers are popular sovereignty and common good of the community	Built on traditional authority, continuity and divine mandate of the King	Built on performance in optimisation and growth
A	Still primitive stage, low professionalisation, diminishing returns on administrative complexity	Efforts to develop a centralised command and control system diminishing returns on complexity	Focus o efficiency, cost-cutting, over-specialisation, silos and audit culture, diminishing returns on complexity
N	Glorification of roman values and roman founders	Sacralisation of the King and his authority	Reconciling new goals with optimisation priority (e.g. green economic growth)
	Q - Quantum Learning block		
	Q transitioning to **"obeying"**	Q transitioning to **"optimising"**	Q transitioning to **"autonomy"**
I	Small share of individuals empowered to control high share of resources, downward socio-economic mobility for high share of individuals, rising allegiance to influential individuals vs community	High gap between reality of capitals and official social stratification system, rising bourgeois class through trade and industry, economic capital increasingly driven by optimisation vs privileges, divergence within privileged orders	Technological disruptions have a magnifying impact on individual's initial stock of capitals and as such potential individual accomplishments, increased individual autonomy via this impact of technology
C	Shift from a small and homogenous community to larger heterogeneous one threat to unity, competing definitions of roman identity	Spread of enlightenment ideals, national awakening around a civic collective identity detached from the person of the King	Rise of post-materialist values, desacralisation of optimisation core beliefs and stakeholders, diversification of societal identities

Source: Whiteshield

with that of the community. The rising differences in economic and cultural capitals between individuals, along with the emergence of competing social meanings, threatened the unity of the community. The Romans who supported Tiberius in large numbers had less and less in common with the senators and thus felt little constraint in opposing them. The increasing importance of individual vs community allegiance also played a significant role given that the first supporters of Tiberius were soldiers serving under him who developed loyalty for him after he protected their lives in the battlefield.

In the case of Camille and Robespierre's story, the gap was between an Energy block which fits in the 2nd age of development and a Quantum Learning block transitioning towards the 3rd age. It is in this context that Camille's speech triggered the storming of the Bastille and in the same context that the National Assembly managed to gain the legitimacy it needed to become the effective government of France. Camille's speech was inspired by Enlightenment ideals which were accessible to him because the individual meaning of the bourgeoisie was increasing economically but also culturally. However, his speech also spoke to individuals of a lower urban and rural class who didn't have such a high level of cultural capital, but their interests aligned with those ideals nonetheless and the strength of their solidarity networks enabled further reach and impact. Their individual meaning was higher than their ancestors' who had no choice but to adhere to the stratified social order. The Assembly was able to rise to the level of effective government because of the divergence of individual meaning between members of privileged orders and the convergence of interests among individuals of the Third Estate. The social meaning on which the 'obeying' policy system was based provided in itself a breeding ground for the social meaning that would enable the Assembly to acquire legitimacy. Indeed, the monarchy had striven to create a collective identity that was centered around the King, but which was civic, nonetheless. Coupled with structural transformations, such as territorial homogenisation and connectedness, the progressive expansion of the French language, and the development of newspapers, this led to the development of a national consciousness, a public opinion and the shift towards a collective identity which remained based on a civic principle but centred around popular sovereignty rather than allegiance to the King.

Finally, in the case of Miremba, the gap was between an Energy block which fits into the 3rd age of development and a Quantum Learning block transitioning towards the 4th age of development. It is in this context that young activists such as Miremba or Greta Thunberg managed to initiate movements, both digital and physical, bringing together millions of individuals across the globe. The impact of technology on their individual meaning is apparent in enabling a high social capital, a mobilisation of financial resources and a higher access to educational resources and knowledge. The dominance of young people in the movement showcased in the story illustrates the generational effect of rising post-materialist values. The global nature of the movement highlights the shift away from prioritisation of national identities. While we have focused in the analysis of this third story on this global aspect and as such on the dominant paradigm, this should not eclipse differences between countries. Indeed, the individual experience of Miremba in her country, as opposed to other activists in developed countries, clearly illustrated that the gap between an autonomy-oriented quantum learning and an optimisation-oriented policy system is not homogeneous across countries. Her struggles in rallying support for the environmental and sustainability cause in her country, as well as the reasons driving this lack of interest, be it a prioritisation of other policy goals or weak knowledge of the subject, show that it is not a homogeneous transition everywhere. Obviously, her peer activists in developed countries, while able to rally more support, still had to face significant opposing voices, a lot of which are founded on the defence of the 'optimising' paradigm of the 3rd age. However, the purpose of this last story was simply to showcase signs of an initial transition and the three stories differ in terms of the intensity of the gap between the Energy and the Quantum Learning blocks and as such the intensity of events and social unrest described in the stories.

2. *There are constants of change*

Our three stories differ significantly in terms of various dimensions. The spatiotemporal contexts are diversified with the first story taking place in the 1st century BC in the Roman Republic, the second set in France in late-18th century and the third set in Switzerland in the current era. The main policy fields around which the stories are centred are also different. In the case of Tiberius, the main policy in question is an economic one of land distribution. In the case of Camille and Robespierre the core nature of the crisis is political and institutional. And finally, in the case of Miremba, the central policy field is environmental and sustainability policy. The nature of events varies from an institutional crisis to a political revolution to a global activism movement.

As highlighted above, we also have a diversity in terms of the paradigms of development ages (1st, 2nd, 3rd, 4th) and societal directions (belonging, obeying, optimising, autonomy). These large differences were intentional in order to highlight that despite them, our stories can be analysed through a common analytical framework based on constants of change. As long as societies exist, we will always have policy systems and networks of individuals as frames of references. And our frameworks should be centred around this interaction between policy systems and the absorption capacity of individuals as the main driver of change rather than assumptions or narratives specific to a certain paradigm which are bound to become irrelevant and narrow our perspectives within a closed system.

3. *It is about the policy mix not the individual policy ingredients*

All three stories have a public policy field or domain. In the case of Tiberius, it was an agrarian land reform. In the case of Camille and Robespierre, it was political representation and the political regime. In the case of Miremba, it was environmental policy. But told back-to-back, these stories highlight that this notion of policy fields is a reductionist chimera. In reality, the agrarian land reform was intrinsically related to the rest of the policy mix. For instance, the impact it had cannot be understood without accounting for the military policy of increasing conquests, military expenses, and the expansion of the pool of citizens drafted into the army which increased the issue of land distribution by sending soldiers on long and distant military campaigns, leading to a deterioration of their farms which would be bought by larger and more competitive land-owners. It is also linked to the labour policy of free person to slave labour substitution which considerably reduced work opportunities for Roman citizens. And it is also linked to the monetary policy where a combination of increased silver supply from Spanish mining and external conquests, revaluations, and decreasing bronze weight standards pushed the Roman price system into an inflationary spiral deepening the socio-economic crisis. Similarly, the political issues at the heart of Camille and Robespierre's story were inseparable from the rest of the policy mix. Be it the military policy which increased the public budget deficit, or in turn the resulting rising tax policy which further worsened the situation of peasants, subject both to feudal fees and government taxes, or the labour policy which didn't have in place any protection mechanism for labourers and workmen whose situation in the urban environment was precarious, or the reforms to decrease subsidies of food products, such as bread, deepening the economic difficulties of the lower class. Finally, Miremba's story further illustrates this point since although the main policy field in question in this story is environmental policy, it is obviously the broader policy mix that matters as highlighted by the activist movement itself advocating for a change of the system rather than new sustainability policies. Environmental policies are inevitably linked to industrial policy, economic regulation, governance, education, social protection, and employment, and the challenges illustrated by the story are linked to the 3rd age policy mix as a whole and not strictly to environmental policy.

4. *Nothing is lost, nothing is created, everything is transformed*
What we mean here is that any energy introduced by the policy system cannot be lost, it can only be transformed. In an ideal scenario of convergence, the energy is converted into the common goals for which it was intended. However, if divergence and inefficiencies occur and the energy is not recovered in the objectives it was intended for, it is not lost but transformed into unintended consequences. For instance, if administrative inefficiencies arise in the implementation of a public policy, the energy introduced can be transformed into a growing mistrust of the public sector or accumulated social unrest and anger. In our second story, several administrative inefficiencies arose from using tax-farming practices to collect taxes, especially indirect ones due to corruption and extorsion of taxpayers, leading to a lower capacity of the state to increase its revenues. This apparent 'loss' of energy was converted into social dissatisfaction especially among the rural lower-class citizens who still had to bear the burden of the taxation policy as administrated by the tax farmers and this would come to play a key role in the inability of the regime to rally support from this population in the events of 1789. Another illustration of our fourth point is the importance of narratives. One might be tempted to dismiss the importance of this variable under the assumption that only actions matter in public policy. But narratives are a form of energy introduced, an energy subject to transformation as well. In the case of divergence between narratives and policy mixes, for instance, the gap between 'words' and 'actions'. The energy introduced by narratives is not lost but susceptible to feed social dissatisfaction. Miremba's story is illustrative of this point. One of the main factors contributing to the rise of the global protest movement in this story, a factor that the movement itself explicitly mentions, is the cognitive dissonance and the gap between, on the one hand narratives of change to adopt sustainable development paradigms

and prioritise environmental goals, and on the other the reality of policy mixes which remain heavily oriented towards the 3rd age of development. Finally, the same can be said about the energy introduced by legitimisation frameworks where divergence leads to energy conversion into unintended consequences. For instance, in Tiberius' story, a foundational pillar of the legitimisation framework of the policy system draws on its contribution to the common good of the community combined with an affirmative legitimisation based on popular sovereignty. When the policy mix did not align with this legitimisation framework, the energy was converted into popular resistance and unrest. This is the reason that enabled Tiberius to gain a significant number of supporters who was using this very legitimisation framework to justify opposition to the Senate and acts which could have been considered as unconstitutional according to the unspoken rules of Roman conduct, such as bypassing the authority of the Senate and deposing an opposing tribune.

5. *Collective memory and tipping points*

A final message to highlight is that the rhythm of change is not always incremental or continuous and tipping points can occur as illustrated by our stories. Various factors can explain these tipping points. Among them is collective memory and circumstantial convergence within networks of individuals based on a common divergence from policy systems.

The case of Tiberius highlights the importance of collective memories. As explained in our story, the events relating to him did not lead to the fall of the Republic. In fact, it would go on to survive for a century. However, it can be considered as a tipping point because of the impact it had on collective memories. Tiberius was the first to break the unspoken rules of conduct in the political arena. None of his acts were illegal per se, but they were uncommon and went against informal institutions deeply rooted in the collective consciousness. His bypassing of the senate, his deposition of an opposing tribune, his attempt to get elected for a second mandate, all infringed on those informal institutions and opened the door to future ones by inscribing in the collective memory the possibility of doing so. Similarly, the reaction of senators to Tiberius also deeply impacted the collective memory by introducing a precedent for violence in politics after Tiberius' assassination and justifying it as acceptable. As such, the combination of these two events and the impact on the collective memory will lead to a century of political violence and the emergence of figures similar to Tiberius in the political scene, ultimately culminating in the fall of the Republic.

On the other hand, the story of Camille and Robespierre illustrates how a tipping point can happen via circumstantial convergence of networks of individuals. By that we mean the convergence of interests of networks which have different individual meanings and would have in other circumstances had divergent interests. But in a specific context these interests can merge when the main common point becomes the divergence from the policy system. Regardless of the differences between the various networks, they agree in their divergence from the policy system as was the case with the significantly diversified networks during the French Revolution (high bourgeoisie, intellectual elite, middle bourgeoise, peasantry, urban workmen, low clergy).

Chapter Three

THE ENERGY OF POLICY SYSTEMS

'The whole is greater than the sum of its parts.' A policy system should be about the mix not the individual ingredients. And some of the ingredients are not even policies.

THE POLICY ENERGY BLOCK

As we have described, the policy Energy block is made up of four components: policy mix optimality (P), legitimacy (L), administrative efficiency (A) and narrative (N).

PUBLIC POLICIES: OPTIMALITY OF THE POLICY MIX

The first factor to investigate in the Energy block is the 'what' of public policies. What policies, what institutions are pursued by countries and policymakers and what conditions their optimality? This is the traditional question extensively addressed by development studies and policy analysis.

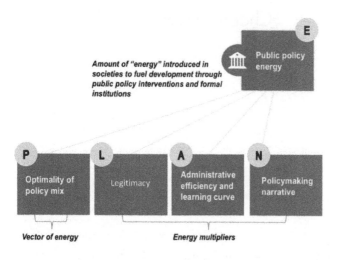

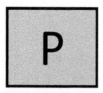

P	Optimality of the policy mix

- The policy mix is the set of policies and institutions used by a country or society.

- Policies do not operate in a vacuum and therefore for policies to have the greatest impact on development the right *mix* of policies must be chosen.

- Public policies and policy goals should be approached as a network where each policy or goal is a node influencing and depending on other nodes.

- A first step in accounting for the optimality of policy mixes is to assess a country's ability to leverage the most influential policies – those with the highest effect when considering network linkages.

A first question that naturally arises when we think about the optimality of the policy mix is: do we know what policies matter? Or alternatively, do we have a sound approach to investigating which policies matter?

As mentioned previously, our knowledge of which factors drive the material development and progress of countries has radically changed throughout time. We are bound to witnessing periodic paradigm changes around key development factors: from free and open markets and sound institutions to strong investments in human capital. Evidently, this is understandable given that our judgement of what works depends on the objectives to achieve, on the set of development goals considered as the 'north' for policymakers, and, as stated earlier, these objectives are continuously changing and not fixed in time.

However, within this evolving process, it is important to understand how we attempt to determine critical policies to focus on and to be aware of the limitations of our approaches. For several decades now, evidence-based policymaking has become the best practice praised by the policymaking realm, an approach summarised by Tony Blair's slogan in the 1990s: 'What matters is what works.'

Several years later and despite rising criticism around this rationalist dream, the idea remains popular, and is advocated by international organisations, think tanks, policy centres, and governmental actors. The concept is gaining new momentum with the advent of big data, and behavioural policy and research movements. While 'what matters is what works' is an appealing movement and one that has certainly contributed to raising the state of our knowledge of public policies, being aware of its limitations is critical. And a major one to overcome is the sectorial or reductionist approach to this question.

As mentioned, the policy landscape still fails to consider the interconnectivity, synergies, trade-offs and complex relationships between different policy fields.

This leads us to our second question: how can we escape from policy silos and investigate public policies in a holistic manner?

To answer this question, let us step back from the realm of policymaking for a moment and consider the example of another field focusing on the building blocks of our world: chemistry. How did we build our knowledge of elements, the fundamental units of matter? How did we manage to obtain and continuously improve a table of elements, classifying them by their properties in the periodic table?

The answer lies in one word: reactions. It is the study of the interactions between different elements that enables us to uncover the inherent properties of each. This is strikingly different to public policy where we continuously attempt, in vain, to isolate 'elements' which are connected in the real world. As such, our focus should shift from individual policy 'ingredients' to linkages and policy mixes. Focusing on policies with little influence or without the right mix can lead to slow or no progress – put simply you will hit a brick wall or glass ceiling.

The Policy Experience Curve

In the following sections we will provide an illustration of how public policies can be approached as a network and how we can enhance our focus on policy mixes. Our framework and model, based on network analysis techniques, can be considered as an example of such a perspective and a first step in exploring analytical tools and frameworks which are more aligned with a holistic policy strategy.

Leveraging network analysis tools, we engaged in studying patterns of policy linkages while disregarding any pre-existing assumption of linearity. The starting point was a network of Sustainable Development Goal (SDG) outcome indicators coupled with a wide range of public policy indicators (see the Methodology box). We started by focusing on two main concepts: the systemic influence of a policy given all the linkages between policies and development outcomes and its systemic dependence on other conditions (be it other policy instruments or policy objectives). The systemic influence is simply defined as the sum of the influence of a policy on all other policies and SDGs in the network. This metric describes the behaviour of a policy from the 'input' perspective: that is, it can be considered as a proxy of the overall effect of the policy on the system given all the linkages it includes. The systemic dependence number is simply defined as the sum of the influence of all other policies and SDGs on the policy of interest. This metric describes the behaviour of a policy from the 'outcome' perspective: that is. it describes to what extent the state of the policy is conditioned by other system variables and by doing so indicates to what extent it would be feasible and relevant to have external intervention targeting direct impact on the policy issue.

Some of the observations derived from this network analysis can be summarised in five main points. First, policy sectors are artificial dichotomies. The traditional hierarchical classification of policy issues by specific silos or sectors – such as education policy, health policy, or environmental policy – is not supported by empirical evidence. Instead, our analysis shows that policy issues are connected across these sectors suggesting that it is more appropriate to approach them as a network of nodes and links revealing potential synergies and trade-offs across sectors. In some cases, policy issues traditionally classified within the same sector can exhibit stronger connections. However, this is not a systemic observation which could justify maintaining the traditional sectorial approach.

Second, the relationship between policy inputs and outcomes is not linear and the distinction between policy inputs and outcomes is relative. The network perspective questions the assumed linearity between policy inputs and outcomes for several reasons. Firstly, and expectedly, a policy outcome can be connected to several inputs including, as established previously, inputs from other policy 'sectors'. Secondly, there is no straightforward distinction between an input and an outcome within the network. Policy outcomes are not exclusively influenced by inputs but also by other outcomes. Thirdly and conversely, policy inputs do not only exclusively influence outcomes but are also dependent both on other inputs and other outcomes. Consequently, what is traditionally considered as an input can be viewed as an outcome in another setting and vice versa.

The experience curve

- **Database:** This includes two types of indicators: SDGs (policy goals) and public policies (policy instruments). The Sustainable Development Agenda includes seventeen goals. Each goal includes a set of targets and each target is measured through a number of indicators. In order to build our dataset, we collected country performance for 151 countries in each indicator passing a data availability threshold of at least 40% coverage for the 151 countries. A ten-year average performance was computed for each country in each indicator. Target scores were assigned to each country by averaging country performance in the indicators included in the SDG target and normalising the final target score on a 1–100 basis. The SDG database was complemented by a policy database. The latter included an exhaustive list of the most common public policies across sectors and the types of policy instruments (e.g. public expenditure on education, legal provisions of gender equality, taxation of corporation). For each policy, countries were provided with a score assessing their average adoption of said policy over the past decade and based on raw data collected from a wide range of recognised sources and international organisations (World Bank, OECD, IMF, UNESCO, WHO, UN DATA, WEF, etc.).

- **Statistical model:** We adopted the dependency network methodology to derive linkages between this set of policy goals and policy instruments. We calculated the partial correlation effect for each node (either an SDG target or a public policy) on all other pairwise correlations in the network. We defined the total influence of node j on node i, $D(i,j)$, as the average influence of node j on the correlations, $C(i,k)$, over all nodes k. The node dependencies define a dependency matrix, D, whose (i,j) element is the influence of node j on node i. It is important to note that the dependency matrix is non-symmetrical since the influence of node j on node i is not equal to the influence of node i on node j.

The experience curve

- **Key metrics:** As such, for each indicator (SDG target or public policy), we were able to derive two main metrics.

(1) The systemic influence (or influence) of each node.
In this approach, the influence of a node j on a node i is defined as the average relative effect of variable j on the correlations $C(i, k)$ over all variables k not equal to i.

- The relative effect of j on the correlation $C(i, k)$ is: $d(i, k \mid j) \equiv C(i, k) - PC(i, k \mid j)$, where $C(i, k)$ is the correlation between variables i and k, and $PC(i, k \mid j)$ is the partial correlation between i and k given j.

- The influence of j on i, $D(i,k)$, is defined as a measure of the average influence of variable j on the correlations $C(i, k)$, over all variables k not equal to j.

$$D(i,j) = \frac{1}{N-1}\sum_{k \neq j}^{N-1} d(i,k \mid j).$$

- The **systemic influence of j**, *SLI(j)*, is defined as the sum of the influence of j on all other variables i not equal to j.

$$SLI\,(j) = \sum_{i \neq j}^{N-1} D(i,j).$$

The systemic influence of j figure

a **Partial Correlation**   **b** **Dependency Matrix**   **c** **Systemic influence**

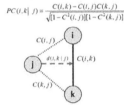

$$PC(i,k \mid j) = \frac{C(i,k) - C(i,j)C(k,j)}{\sqrt{[1 - C^2(i,j)][1 - C^2(k,j)]}}$$

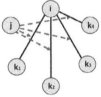

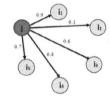

The correlation influence

$d(i,k \mid j) \equiv C(i,k) - PC(i,k \mid j)$

$$D(i,j) = \frac{1}{N-1}\sum_{k=j}^{N-1} d(i,k \mid j)$$

Systemic influence $(j) = \sum_{i=j}^{N-1} D(i,j) = 3.1$

(2) The systemic dependence (or dependence) of each node.
Since, the dependency matrix is non-symmetrical, we can also sum all the influences (or dependencies) of all other nodes i in the network on node j – $D(j,i)$, that is the systemic dependence.

Third, policies are not equal due to differences in systemic influence and systemic dependence. The network approach reveals that policies are connected and that some policies inherently have a higher systemic influence meaning that progress in these specific policy issues would percolate through the network and enable stronger overall impact. Just as the systemic influence of policies is not equal, their systemic dependence is not either. Some policy issues inherently exhibit higher levels of dependency on other variables in the system. This can be interpreted in two ways. Firstly, the systemic dependence can reveal to what extent it would be relatively easy or difficult to induce progress in a given policy issue through exogenous interventions. Externally inducing progress for a policy issue which is heavily dependent on several other variables would be more difficult since the effectiveness of such external intervention can be conditioned by the state of the other variables on which the policy is dependent. Secondly, the notion of systemic dependence can also give a sense of cost of opportunity in the context of resources optimisation where external interventions for policy issues with low systemic dependence would be more relevant than in the case of policy issues with high systemic dependence since progress in the latter could be achieved endogenously through network efforts between policies.

An interesting example highlighted in our results is the case of education and education policy. Intuitively, and based on the importance of education and human capital in our policy systems, one could expect education policies including public investments and expenditure on education to rank as highly influential policies in the policy network. However, our research highlights that most education expenditure policies belong to the lower-influence groups of policies and this finding holds when segregating such policies by levels of education (pre-primary, primary, secondary, tertiary). Education outcomes on the other hand, such as completion rates and Programme for International Student Assessment (PISA) scores, as expected, hold a highly influential position in the network with linkages spanning across policy sectors. Digging deeper on key factors influencing performance in these outcomes, the network reveals the importance of less obvious policy choices such as gender policy, governance and public administration (including government accountability, regulatory enforcement and even decentralisation) as well as public expenditure in other sectors such as social protection.

Fourth, our experience curve, which maps the systemic influence and systemic dependence of public policies shows that there is a strong relationship between these two metrics (Figure 20). A major implication of this is non-substitutability and the importance of policy paths adopted by countries, meaning that countries cannot skip stages to adopt the most influential policies if those inherently require more connections. Systemic dependence can be interpreted as a proxy for integration requirements in the policy network. Policies with a high systemic dependence are those which require to be highly integrated in the network and as such necessitate extensive coordination efforts. Therefore, it appears that higher integration and coordination of

Figure 20.   Modelised experience curve of public policies

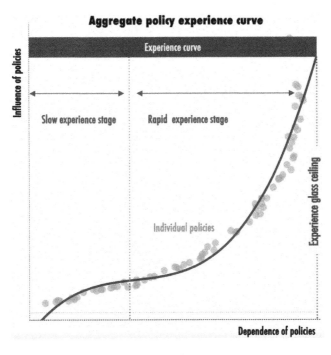

Source: Whiteshield

policies is associated with a higher overall effect on the network. This further
sustains the need to focus on policy mixes and adopt a network perspective.
Consider, for instance, two policies included in our database: introducing a
consumption tax and enhancing regulatory enforcement, which differ significantly in their levels of systemic influence and dependence. Intuitively, one
would expect the integration needs of a policy such as regulatory enforcement to be much greater than a more instrumental type of policy such as the
introduction of a consumption tax, given that it should require a broader
spectrum of conditions to be effectively adopted. And that is indeed the case,
with the introduction of a consumption tax falling at the bottom of our experience curve while enhancing regulatory enforcement is situated at the top
of the curve (Figure 21). However, this positioning should be not perceived
as strictly static. The systemic influence and dependence of a policy can be
changed. Indeed, the position of a specific public policy on the experience

Figure 21.   Computed experience curve of public policies

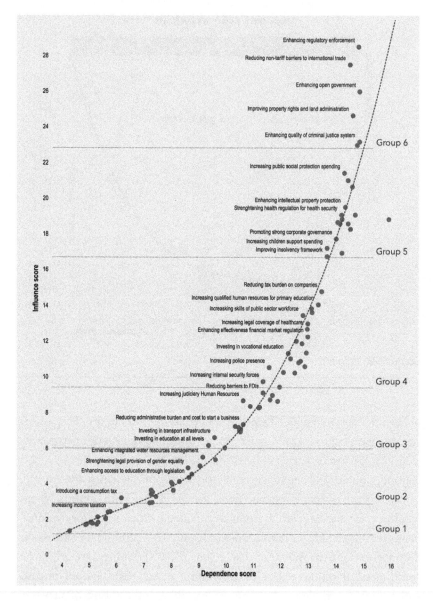

Source: Whiteshield

curve appears to depend on different drivers. Some of these drivers are inherent to the policy: certain public policies are bound to be more connected and have a higher effect given a set of development goals. But other drivers are linked to time, experience or strategy dimensions. For instance, as the range of policy instruments expands over time, newly introduced policies have a margin of improvement and their position along the curve can evolve until reaching a saturation stage which reflects the maximum potential inherent to a given policy. Policies of a more instrumental nature, such as the example of a consumption tax, and which initially fall into a low influence, low dependence zone of the curve can still gain in influence if policy strategies ensure a better integration into the network and alignment with other policies to further enhance their influence.

Fifth, this relationship between influence and dependence, as depicted by the experience curve, is not constant. It follows three main stages; a slow experience stage where an increase in dependence leads to a less then proportional increase in influence; a rapid experience stage with increasing marginal returns on policy dependence; and a stagnation phase materialised by an experience saturation or glass ceiling. These stages allow us to differentiate between three groups of policies (Figure 22). Firstly, dependent policies for which the ratio of systemic influence over systemic dependence (impact score) is inferior to 1. The integration needs for these policies are higher than the overall effect derived from them. Secondly, influential policies for which the ratio of systemic influence over systemic dependence is higher than 1. And finally, the highly influential policies. The ratio of systemic influence over systemic dependence is situated between 1.5 and 2. A ratio of 2 seems to be the glass ceiling indicating that these policies are close to the maximal influence that can be derived given network conditions.

The Periodic Table of Public Policies

Digging deeper into the patterns of policy linkages revealed by the network analysis, it appears that the behaviour of policies follows a periodic logic that can be summarised in two concepts: the systemic influence of the policy and the concentration of said influence in the policy network. This pattern allows us to map a periodic table of public policies following the same spirit as the periodic table of chemical elements.

Figure 22.   Policy scores in influence, dependence and impact metrics

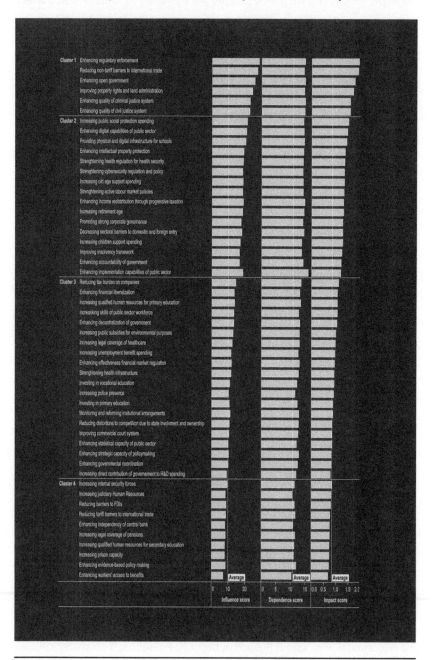

Figure 22. (Continued)

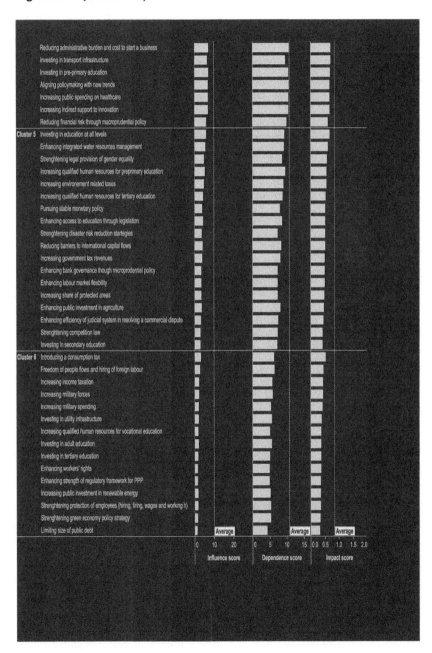

Source: Whiteshield

In the atomic representation, each shell of the atom can contain a specific number of electrons before it becomes saturated. The electrons then move to the following shell and fill it until this new layer becomes saturated itself. The number of shells is represented by the rows or periods in periodic table while the number of electrons in the last shell is captured by the columns or groups. In our policy representation, each shell of the policy can be conceived as a zone of the policy's influence in the network. A policy with a high number of shells is one which its effect is spread across a high number of nodes in the network. A policy with a low number of shells is one which its effect is concentrated in a few nodes only. The number of electrons in the shell can be conceived as the intensity of the effect of a policy (the systemic influence). The combinations then vary from a low systemic influence spread across a high number of nodes to a high systemic influence concentrated in a few nodes (Figure 23).

As such, the groups in our table classify policies by the intensity of their effect (systemic influence) while the periods classify them according to the concentration of said influence in the policy network. Finally, the blocks of the table combine both criteria to group policies. Six main blocks of policies emerge ranging from light policies with low influence and high concentration to heavy policies with high influence and low concentration (Figure 24). Similarly to elements in the chemical periodic table, new policies can be added to the table, as policymakers are confronted by new challenges and need new tools to resolve them. Additionally, the position of a public policy in the periodic table is not immutable. Changing priorities in terms of policy goals, enhanced experience in the policy design and implementation, emergence of new challenges and new public policies are all factors that can contribute to changing the position of a certain policy in the periodic table.

A key message highlighted both by the periodic table and the influence/dependence curve is the fact that the classification of public policies along policy domains, such as education and economy, is not substantial. It cannot help us derive insights on policy strategies. In both models, no specific pattern related to policy domains can be detected in terms of influence, dependence or influence concentration. In other words, policies at the top or at the bottom of the influence/dependence curve and in block 1 or block 6 of the periodic table can be from the same policy domains.

This points to the importance of using alternative policy classifications which can help derive strategic policy insights. To illustrate how our two

Figure 23.   Graphical representation of the two metrics of the periodic table

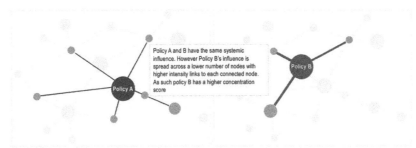

Size of bubbles indicates systemic influence. Width of links indicates scale of influence on connected node

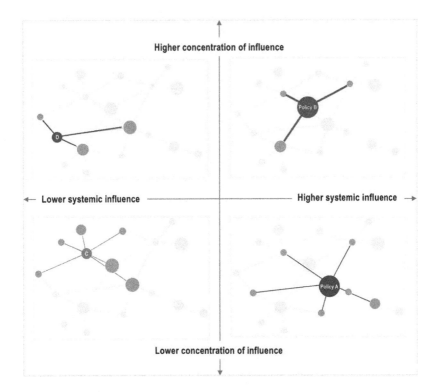

Source: Whiteshield

models can help us do that, we will take the example of one of the policies included in our database: enhancing regulatory enforcement (Figure 25 is the policy presentation based on the two models). This policy falls at the top

Figure 24.   Modelised periodic table of public policies

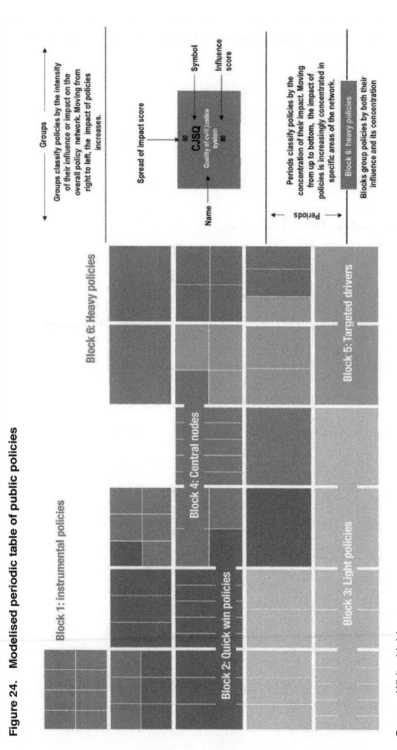

Source: Whiteshield

Figure 25.   Individual policy page – Case of enhancing regulatory enforcement policy (RE)

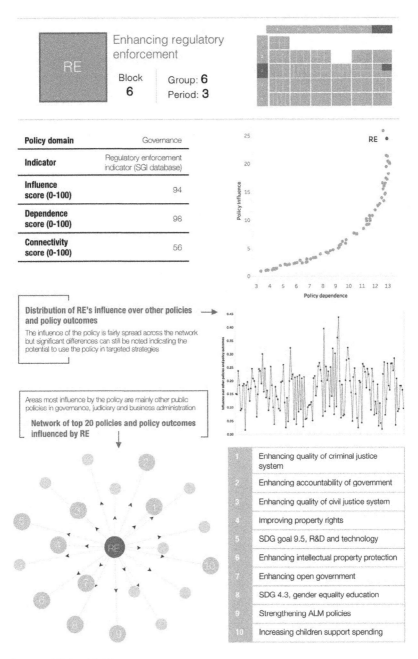

Source: Whiteshield

of the influence/dependence curve meaning it has a large impact on the network of public policies and policy outcomes, but that impact is conditioned by a large number of policy factors. This makes it a prime candidate for prioritisation and integration. Its high dependence means that policy efforts to enhance regulatory enforcement need a significant level of coordination across policy domains but once achieved, it has the potential to unlock progress in a wide range of policy areas. It is situated in block 6 of the periodic table which includes policies with high influence and medium-to-low concentration meaning the policy should have a high effect spread across a relatively large share of the policy network. Digging deeper into the network of policy areas most impacted by the policy in question helps us uncover that enhancing regulatory enforcement acts primarily as an enabler of other public policies such as the quality of the judiciary process, and the improvement of property rights or government accountability, compared to other policies whose influence is concentrated directly on policy goals, in our case, SDGs. This means that weaknesses in regulatory enforcement can act as obstacles in the success of other policies and entails the need to consider this specific policy as a stepping stone and to take it into account in the design and implementation of other public policies.

The periodic table of public policies	Methodology

- **Methodology and database:** The periodic table of public policies relies on the same database and network analysis as the experience curve of public policies (see experience curve methodology box).
- **Key metrics:** The periodic table relies on two main metrics to classify public policies.
    1. **The systemic influence of a policy:** This is defined as the sum of the influence of the policy on all other nodes of the policy network (see experience curve methodology box).
    2. **The influence concentration of a policy:** This is measured by the coefficient of variation of the influence of a policy on all the other nodes of the network. A higher coefficient of variation means higher variability of the influence of a policy and suggests higher concentration of its effect on specific nodes of the network rather than a homogeneous effect across the network.

(Continued)

(*Continued*)

- **Conceptual grouping:**

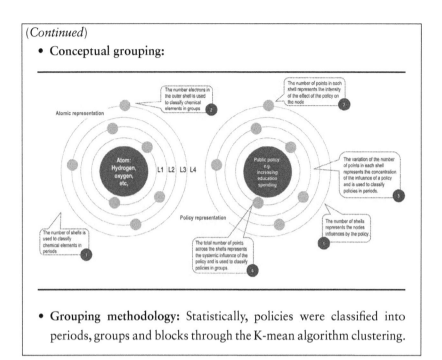

- **Grouping methodology:** Statistically, policies were classified into periods, groups and blocks through the K-mean algorithm clustering.

In order to give a broader picture of our periodic table of public policies, we will introduce the 6 blocks that it includes.

Block 1 (Figure 26) includes policies with a relatively *low influence and a low-to-medium concentration of influence*, meaning they are spread more or less evenly across the policy network. In terms of policy domains, block 1 of the periodic table is relatively diversified and includes green and environmental domain, taxation, labour, and monetary policies. Two important patterns can be highlighted by this block. Firstly, the lack of integration of relatively new policies. Although diversified in terms of policy domains, the block includes a fairly high share of policies related to the environmental and green economy domain which can be considered as one of the more recent policy fields. This suggests that these policies, for instance strengthening green economy strategy, increasing public investment in renewable energy or increasing the share of protected areas, have not yet been fully integrated into the policy network, and as coordination efforts increase, with more experience, their position in the periodic table could potentially change towards higher influence and/or concentration of influence. Secondly, the changing position of policies with shift in societal priorities and development paradigms. This point is particularly illustrated by the positioning of the 'increasing military spending' policy in the low influence, low concentration block.

Figure 26.   Presentation of block 1 of the periodic table of public policies

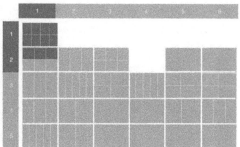

Block 1

Instrumental policies

- Relatively low influence and a low to medium concentration of influence
- New policies which require moving up along the experience curve to gain in influence
- Old policies loosing in influence due to changing priorities
- Influence depends more on the performance in the rest of policies included in the network rather than inherent to them

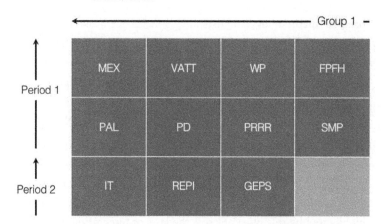

Group 1

MEX	VATT	WP	FPFH
PAL	PD	PRRR	SMP
IT	REPI	GEPS	

Period 1

Period 2

Code	Policy	Concentration score	Influence score
FPFH	Freedom of people flows and hiring of foreign labour	29.13	4.71
GEPS	Strenghtening green economy policy strategy	39.80	1.33
IT	Increasing income taxation	42.49	5.01
MEX	Increasing military spending	10.53	4.08
PAL	Increasing share of protected areas	24.99	5.65
PD	Limiting size of public debt	30.11	0.00
PPPR	Enhancing strength of regulatory framework for PPP	30.86	0.94
REPI	Increasing public investment in renewable energy	37.62	0.63
SMP	Pursuing stable monetary policy	24.24	8.64
VATT	Introducing a consumption tax	18.48	5.00
WP	Strenghtening protection of employees	0.00	1.78

Source: Whiteshield

It is easy to imagine that if we reproduce the periodic table in for an earlier time, decades or even centuries ago, this policy would have belonged to another block given that military-related goals used to have a higher priority and as military-related policies were more integrated into the policy network. Finally, policies which belong to block 1 and fit neither the first nor the second pattern described above, such as increasing income taxation or pursuing a stable monetary policy, can be considered as 'instrumental' policies whose influence depends more on their performance in the rest of policies included in the network rather than inherently in themselves.

Block 2 (Figure 27) includes policies *with a low-to-medium influence and a medium concentration of influence*. These policies can be described as quick win strategies. Although their influence is relatively limited, the low-to-medium concentration means they can quickly spread across the policy network and act as a general enabler by unlocking potential progress across the network. Here again, block 2 is quite diversified in terms of policy domains including education, economy, gender equality and labour policy. But a dominant pattern in terms of the type of policy instruments can be detected. Indeed, the block includes two main types of policy instruments: regulatory ones and public expenditure ones.

The former includes policies such as reducing administrative burdens and costs to start a business, reducing barriers to FDIs, enhancing access to education through legislation, and strengthening legal provision of gender equality. The latter includes initiatives such as investing in secondary education and investing in pre-primary education. On their own, these regulatory and financial instruments cannot guarantee a large influence, but they can unlock several opportunities across a wide range of policy areas and their relatively low dependence on other policy conditions suggests lower requirements which justifies their adoption as quick win strategies.

Block 3 (Figure 28) of the periodic table includes policies with *low-to-medium influence and medium-to-high influence concentration*. Policies included in this block can be divided into three main groups. Firstly, policies that can be considered as targeted policy instruments, that is public policies with a highly concentrated influence in specific areas. These can be leveraged to enhance progress for a specific policy goal or priority rather than across the policy network. Examples include increasing human resources for pre-primary education or enhancing effectiveness of financial market regulation. Secondly, there are newly prioritised policies which may witness a change

Figure 27.   Presentation of block 2 of the periodic table of public policies

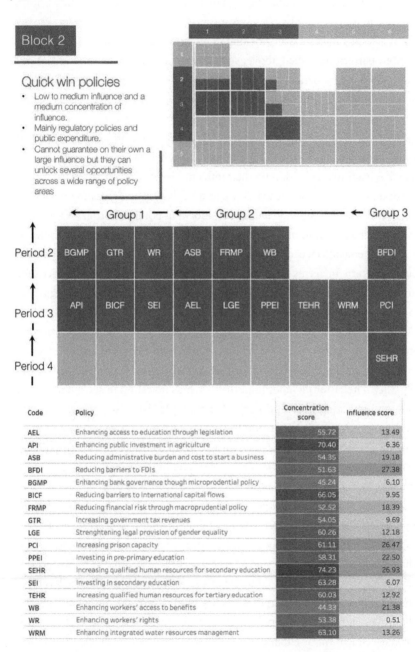

Code	Policy	Concentration score	Influence score
AEL	Enhancing access to education through legislation	55.72	13.49
API	Enhancing public investment in agriculture	70.40	6.36
ASB	Reducing administrative burden and cost to start a business	54.35	19.18
BFDI	Reducing barriers to FDIs	51.63	27.38
BGMP	Enhancing bank governance though microprodential policy	45.24	6.10
BICF	Reducing barriers to international capital flows	66.05	9.95
FRMP	Reducing financial risk through macroprudential policy	52.52	18.39
GTR	Increasing government tax revenues	54.05	9.69
LGE	Strenghtening legal provision of gender equality	60.26	12.18
PCI	Increasing prison capacity	61.11	26.47
PPEI	Investing in pre-primary education	58.31	22.50
SEHR	Increasing qualified human resources for secondary education	74.23	26.93
SEI	Investing in secondary education	63.28	6.07
TEHR	Increasing qualified human resources for tertiary education	60.03	12.92
WB	Enhancing workers' access to benefits	44.33	21.38
WR	Enhancing workers' rights	53.38	0.51
WRM	Enhancing integrated water resources management	63.10	13.26

Source: Whitesheld

Figure 28.   Presentation of block 3 of the periodic table of public policies

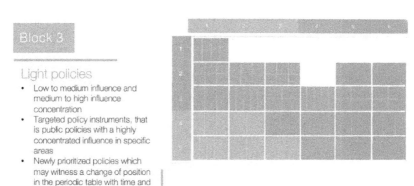

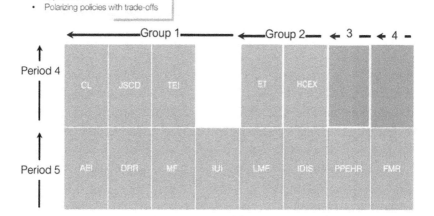

Code	Policy	Concentration score	Influence score
AEI	Investing in adult education	89.8	1.8
CL	Strenghtening competition law	83.7	7.0
DRR	Strenghtening disaster risk reduction startegies	91.6	7.7
ET	Increasing environment related taxes	81.2	14.4
FMR	Enhancing effectiveness financial market regulation	101.7	33.6
HCEX	Increasing public spending on healthcare	82.9	17.2
IDIS	Increasing indirect support to innovation	96.9	20.0
IUI	Investing in utility infrastructure	118.3	2.0
JSCD	Enhancing efficiency of judicial system in commercial disputes	84.4	8.7
LMF	Enhancing labour market flexbility	113.4	6.3
MF	Increasing military forces	98.4	5.1
PPEHR	Increasing qualified human resources for preprimary education	87.9	16.5
TEI	Investing in tertiary education	84.8	0.9

Source: Whiteshield

of position in the periodic table with time and experience. Two interesting examples are investments in adult education and environment-related taxes.

The former shows a relatively low influence but a maximum concentration which can suggest that moving up along the experience curve, this policy can gain more influence and become a targeted policy strategy. The latter shows higher influence and higher spread of influence over the network suggesting that as environmental policies become more integrated and coordinated with the rest of the policy network, this policy can become a systemic driver. Finally, there is the third group includes policies which can be considered as 'polarising' meaning that their high concentration of influence can lead to potential trade-offs and conflicting priorities. A typical example included in the block is enhancing labour market flexibility.

Block 4 (Figure 29) of the periodic table includes policies *with a medium-to-high influence and a medium concentration of influence*. These can be considered as the central nodes which shape the policy system. They include mainly social drivers, economic drivers and a few governance policies. The social drivers include policies such as healthcare access, pension policy or unemployment benefits. The economic drivers cover the key parameters of the economic framework including corporate taxation, financial liberalisation, international trade liberalisation or the commercial judiciary system. The governance policies included in the block are related to the decentralisation of government, and the skills and capabilities of the public sector. These policies define the key features of current policy systems with high influence spread across the network of policy goals.

Block 5 (Figure 30) of the periodic table *includes policies with a high influence and a medium-to-high concentration of influence*. These can be leveraged as targeted policy strategies given that their high impact is concentrated on specific policy areas. The block showcases a relatively strong dominance of corporate, innovation and digital policies such as insolvency and corporate governance regulation, intellectual property, cybersecurity or digital infrastructure for schools. Two main interpretations can be made for these policies. The first relates to policy instruments which are inherently bound to have a concentrated influence given their specificity to a particular cluster. The example of corporate governance most likely falls under this category. The second is linked to policies which currently belong to this block of targeted drivers but can evolve in the future to become systemic drivers meaning that their high influence spreads more evenly across a wider

Figure 29.   Presentation of block 4 of the periodic table of public policies

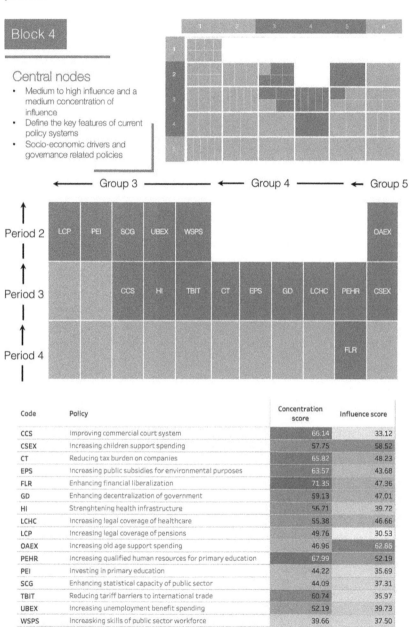

Code	Policy	Concentration score	Influence score
CCS	Improving commercial court system	66.14	33.12
CSEX	Increasing children support spending	57.75	58.52
CT	Reducing tax burden on companies	65.82	48.23
EPS	Increasing public subsidies for environmental purposes	63.57	43.68
FLR	Enhancing financial liberalization	71.35	47.36
GD	Enhancing decentralization of government	59.13	47.01
HI	Strenghtening health infrastructure	56.71	39.72
LCHC	Increasing legal coverage of healthcare	55.38	46.66
LCP	Increasing legal coverage of pensions	49.76	30.53
OAEX	Increasing old age support spending	46.96	62.86
PEHR	Increasing qualified human resources for primary education	67.99	52.19
PEI	Investing in primary education	44.22	35.69
SCG	Enhancing statistical capacity of public sector	44.09	37.31
TBIT	Reducing tariff barriers to international trade	60.74	35.97
UBEX	Increasing unemployment benefit spending	52.19	39.73
WSPS	Increasking skills of public sector workforce	39.66	37.50

Source: Whiteshield

Figure 30.   Presentation of block 5 of the periodic table of public policies

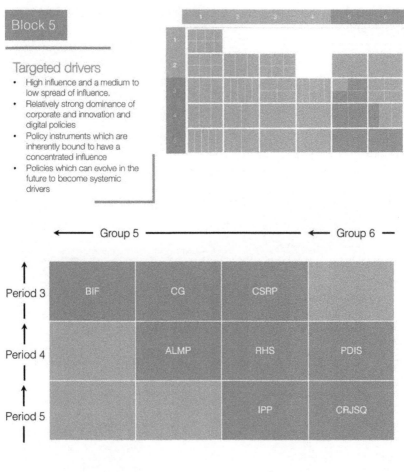

Code	Policy	Concentration score	Influence score
ALMP	Strenghtening active labour market policies	74.50	54.77
BIF	Improving insolvency framework	60.30	60.79
CG	Promoting strong corporate governance	62.67	62.63
CRJSQ	Enhancing quality of criminal justice system	88.95	76.54
CSRP	Strenghtening cybersecurity regulation and policy	64.49	66.35
IPP	Enhancing intellectual property protection	100.47	55.59
PDIS	Providing physical and digital infrastructure for schools	78.52	69.56
RHS	Strenghtening health regulation for health security	73.82	65.46

Source: Whiteshield

range of policy areas. Examples such as technology-related policies have the potential to witness such a transition as transformations related to the digital economy increase in intensity.

Finally, Block 6 (Figure 31) *includes policies with a high influence and low concentration of influence*. These can be considered as heavy policies, the systemic drivers which represent the core fundamentals of the policy system. As such it is unsurprising to detect a high dominance of governance-related policies in this block. Examples include enhancing regulatory enforcement, increasing public sector capabilities and enhancing open and accountable governance. Other policies included in this block relate to the basic principles of current societal and policy paradigms. Relevant examples are the improvement of property rights and the quality of civil justice systems. These policies, with their high influence and low concentration are the breeding ground of more targeted policies such as those included in block 5 and the central nodes of the block 4.

Measuring the Optimality of the Policy Mix

Building on the tools introduced above and the analysis presented, four key factors should be considered in the analysis of the optimality of a policy mix.

Firstly, let us consider development goals. The optimality of a policy mix is relative to a specific set of objectives. Changing the objectives, or the 'north', changes the optimality of the policy mix. As we take the 'north' to be the Sustainable Development Agenda, the optimality of the policy mix should be assessed in reference to this.

Secondly, there are the inherent linkages between various public policies and sustainable development outcomes, as shown by the experience curve and the periodic table of public policies. The focus should be on the policy mix rather than individual policy instruments. Questioning traditional policy silos is fundamental given these linkages between policy instruments and policy goals across traditional sectors. Additionally, and as showcased by our experience curve, higher integration in the policy network is associated with higher influence on the overall network.

Thirdly, consider non-substitutability of policies. As showcased by the experience curve of public policies, policy instruments which tend to have a higher influence on the policy network also require more integration

Figure 31.   Presentation of block 6 of the periodic table of public policies

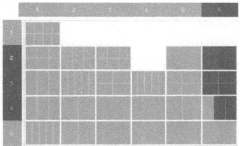

Block 6

Heavy policies

- High influence and high spread of impact.
- Systemic drivers which represent the core fundamentals of the policy system.
- High dominance of governance-related policies
- Breeding ground of more targeted policies such as those included in the 5th block and the central nodes of the 4th block.

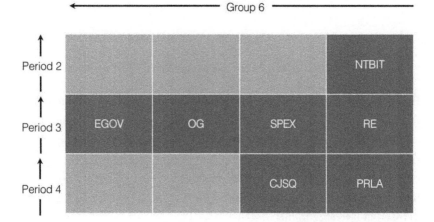

Code	Policy	Concentration score	Influence score
CJSQ	Enhancing quality of civil justice system	79.75	77.60
EGOV	Enhancing digital capabilities of public sector	64.39	78.49
NTBIT	Reducing non-tariff barriers to international trade	51.01	100.00
OG	Enhancing open government	68.20	81.87
PRLA	Improving property rights and land administration	75.13	82.51
RE	Enhancing regulatory enforcement	64.89	94.50
SPEX	Increasing public social protection spending	58.11	74.42

Source: Whiteshield

and coordination. As such, countries cannot skip stages to adopt the most influential policies if these are dependent on other key initial conditions. Additionally, an important characteristic highlighted by the periodic table of public policies is the difference between systemic enablers and more targeted drivers. Some public policies have an influence that is spread fairly evenly across the policy network while others showcase a concentrated influence over a set of specific policies. These differences should be leveraged depending on the policy strategy and the goal at hand.

Fourthly, there is country-specific policy context. Evidently, the optimality of the policy mix varies from one society to another depending on their progress on the development goals. The optimal policy mix of a country is one that not only leverages linkages of policies but also the strengths or comparative advantages of a country to improve key weaknesses.

In our modelling exercise, where we relied on the Sustainable Development Agenda as the definition of the development vision, we adopted two main approaches to attempt an assessment of the optimality of policy mixes, an area which requires further sustained research efforts to get closer to relevant assessment tools. The first approach relied on a global perspective of the optimality of the policy mix drawing on our network analysis and the experience curve of public policies (see the optimality of the policy mix methodology box). The second approach adopted a more country-specific perspective where the optimality of the policy mix can be compared to a constrained optimisation exercise: optimising progress in weakness areas under two types of constraints (1) inherent linkages between policies, (2) strengths and current capabilities of countries.

Optimality of the policy mix   **Methodology**

Database: The same database as the experience curve of public policies (see experience curve methodology box).

Definition of optimality of the policy mix: The ability to leverage policies which maximise returns on the policy network (systemic influence) while minimising integration requirements (systemic dependence), that is to say policies with the highest systemic influence over systemic dependence ratio.

Formula: For a country x, the optimality of the policy mix is computed as:

$$policy\ mix = \sum_{i=1}^{N} Score\ in\ policy\ i \times Impact\ of\ policy\ i$$

$$Impact\ of\ policy\ i = \frac{Systemic\ influence\ of\ i}{Systemic\ dependence\ on\ i} = \frac{\sum_{i \neq j}^{N-1} D(j,i)}{\sum_{i \neq j}^{N-1} D(i,j)}$$

where i (1, N) are the policies of the database.

- The adoption score was defined by following two approaches. In the continuous approach, the adoption score is simply the performance of the country in the policy in question as collected in the database. In the binary approach, the adoption score takes a value of 0 or 1 depending on whether the country showcases a revealed comparative advantage (RCA) in the policy in question. A country has an RCA in the policy if its performance in the policy is higher than the median country performance in this policy and if it is higher than its own median performance across all policies of the database.

- The systemic influence and systemic dependence numbers are derived from the network analysis and the experience curve (see experience curve methodology box).

- No efforts to impute missing values were made.

Focusing on the first approach, the optimality of the policy mix is measured as the ability of countries to leverage policies with the highest systemic influence given policy dependence, that is policies with the highest return on integration efforts. The ratio of systemic influence over systemic dependence from our network analysis is thus used to identify these policies. Two main findings can be highlighted from the application of this methodology to our country and policy database.

The first finding is in terms of the relationship between the optimality of the policy mix and a key input that is the public budget. It appears that the resources of the policy system as proxied by public budget data, do play an important role in the optimality of the policy mix, as would be expected. However, where a high public budget is associated with a high optimality of the policy mix this relationship has several limitations. Firstly, our results showcase

Figure 32.   Relationship between optimality of the policy mix and public budget

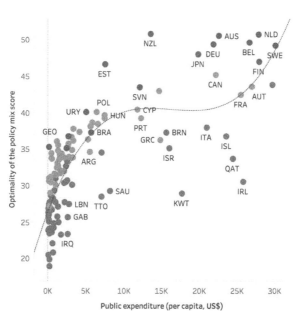

Source: Whiteshield

a relatively high number of countries which are over-performing or under-performing in terms of policy optimality given their levels of public budgets (Figure 32). Secondly, the relationship between public budget and optimality of the policy mix only holds for large differences in public budgets (Figure 33). Indeed, when focusing on more homogeneous groups of countries in terms of public budget, the explanatory power of this variable tends to decrease considerably. As such, while access to higher financial resources can help policy systems to adopt more optimal mixes, the allocation of these resources and the various factors which shape the quality of this allocation matter significantly.

The second finding relates to the relationship between the optimality of the policy mix and development performance. As expected, the model showcases a strong and positive relationship where higher optimality scores are associated with a higher performance in the SDGs (Figure 34). However, it is important to note that several countries are over- or under-performing in SDGs given their optimality of the policy mix, thus confirming that even though a focus on policy mixes and policy linkages is important to capture

Figure 33.   Scatter plots of optimality of the policy mix and public budget by budget levels (from low to high)

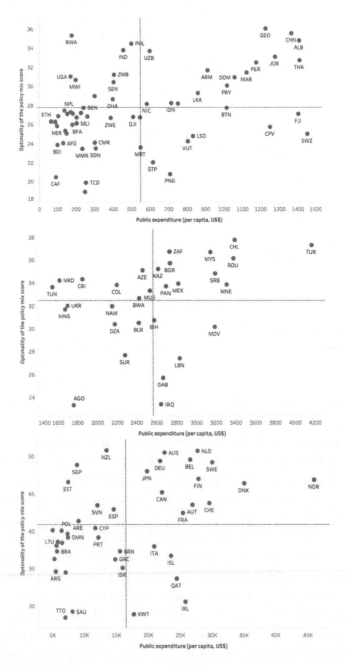

key development inputs, it is not enough to fully account for differences in performance and other aspects of policy systems should be included in development strategies. Moreover, the relationship between our optimality variable and SDG performance displays a concave feature with diminishing marginal returns which confirms this idea of a development glass ceiling when restricting development inputs to technical policy instruments.

Figure 34. Relationship between optimality of the policy mix and SDG performance

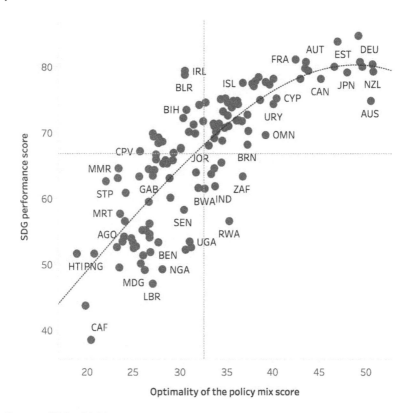

Source: Whiteshield

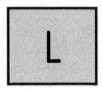

LEGITIMACY: SOUND FOUNDATIONS

In addition to the optimality of the chosen policy mix, other variables can act as multipliers of the 'energy' derived from it. These dimensions are usually underestimated compared to the types of public policies put in place, but they can have an equally important impact. More specifically, three key factors can act as policy 'energy' accelerators, the first of which is legitimacy.

L	Legitimacy

- The first policy energy multiplier is legitimacy. Legitimacy is the glue that binds together the policy system and the network of individuals. Policymakers who face a legitimacy crisis will struggle to gain traction with their initiatives with high implementation, enforcement and transaction costs.

- Legitimacy depends on a wide range of factors including citizen expectations, cultural factors, performance of policymakers, alignment between the values of policymakers and individuals, and efforts to engage citizens in the policymaking process.

- Legitimacy can be quantified through proxy outcome measures such as trust in policymakers.

Political legitimacy is subject to considerable debate. First, there is the question of whether political legitimacy is a descriptive or normative concept. If we consider it to be a descriptive concept, then it is referring to people's beliefs about political authority and obligations. German sociologist Max Weber has written at length on the subject of legitimacy and the role of beliefs. His work is known for distinguishing between the three sources of legitimate rule: tradition, charisma and legal. Individuals can have faith in a political system because it has been around for a considerable amount of time or has simply always existed (tradition), believe in a leader due to their unique qualities and/or commitment to the nation (charisma) or for the final reason of trusting its legitimacy in law (legal–rational).[1] These concepts are dynamic, that is they change over time. For instance, if a charismatic leaders passes away and the next in line does not have the charisma or personality to match then tradition or a legal framework may be used to create the image of legitimacy.

If we are to conceive political legitimacy as a normative concept, then this view is incorrect. Instead, political legitimacy is perceived as a standard of acceptability or justification of political power or authority. There is some ambiguity regarding the definition of legitimacy as a normative concept and there are differing opinions among academics and theorists. Some link legitimacy and justice as combined concepts while others believe they are related but are different domains.[2] Social contracts form an important part of normative legitimacy.

Every public policy can be approached as a form of contract between policymakers and individuals. This contract engages a reciprocity relationship where individuals accept the need to make sacrifices, to pay a certain price in exchange for what they receive from the public policy in question. This contractual relationship entails a level of trust, which can be seen as a proxy for legitimacy in the normative sense. Therefore, a key determinant of policymakers' ability to enact their strategies is trust. In this respect trust is a policy multiplier.

The **importance of legitimacy and trust is not exclusive to the policymaker– citizen relationship,** it is important across all human relationships. Trust is at the core of many everyday relationships and the examples are infinite: employer–employee, supplier–contractor, school–parent, doctor–patient, the list can go on and on. If we take as an example the doctor–patient relationship, trust is essential on both sides: trust from the patient that they will receive confidential and accurate advice or support and the doctor must trust that their patient is truthful and honest. Asymmetric information is present and in these situations trust is key. The patient does not have the knowledge to treat themselves and the doctor does not truly know the legitimacy of the information being provided, hence trust is needed to counteract the level of unequal knowledge. A lack of trust in this scenario can have a devastating impact. One example of what can happen when the trust breaks is the rise in the 'anti-vaxxer' movement that has occurred in recent years. Individuals who chose not to vaccinate themselves or their children believe there is reason to distrust the information they receive from the healthcare sector. This is a clear example of a reduction in trust between patients, or those acting on their behalf, and the healthcare sector. In some cases, third parties, such as the World Health Organisation, must act as intermediaries to improve the level of trust between the parties involved.[3] There is early evidence which suggests that when there is more trust between patient and doctor health outcomes are improved.[4]

Trust can decrease the need for coercion and subsequently reduces the transaction and enforcement costs. It also limits free-riding and opportunistic behaviour. A recent example is the use of masks in response to COVID-19. In some countries, simply asking citizens to wear a mask was enough to enact a change in behaviour, whereas in others there was a need for fines, legal ultimatums and punishment. Similar parallels can be drawn between levels of tax avoidance, traffic regulation compliance and the aforementioned vaccination rate. In many nations, managing compliance with tax regulations is a core component of modern regulation enforcement. There are varying degrees of tax compliance across the globe. In academic literature there are two main theories as to why tax evasion occurs: the rational choice theory and the role of attitudes and moral obligations. In rational choice theory an individual or company is weighing up their options and constructing their decision on the risk and economic reward of non-compliance. Their decision is motivated purely by the economic analysis of the tax conundrum. However, this theory fails to consider the real-world context in which the decision is made and ignores the moral and social obligation an individual may feel about compliance. An individual may hold strong beliefs about doing the right thing (i.e. compliance) and may not want to deal with the social repercussions of being caught avoiding tax, irrespective of the financial benefit tax avoidance may bring. In recent years, there has been an increased focus on the role trust plays in the fabric of compliance with rules and regulations. Research by Murphy (2004) strengthens the argument for trust to be considered as a component of tax compliance. The work explicitly states that strategies aimed at reducing levels of distrust between taxpayers and regulatory bodies may prove effective in gaining voluntary compliance.[5]

Policymakers are responsible for leading reform and **trust can play an essential role in making reform happen.** It can be guaranteed that almost every reform will have winners and losers and every change will lead to short-term sacrifices for long-term benefits. Reforms that face strong opposition from citizens or business denote, first and foremost, of a lack of trust. If we did not trust a business to deliver goods when purchased, we would not order from them. This analogy has implications for government. A lack of trust between citizens and policymakers suggests that individuals do not believe the benefits promised will be fulfilled and therefore are not open to the prospect of reform. One clear example of where trust in future outcomes is needed is pension reform. When enacting pension reform, change will be needed in the here and now but the benefits will not be realised for years or decades to come. In France, President Macron is attempting to bring forward pension reform which he states will be fairer and less complex. However, the reform has been met with considerable opposition from the French people. An IFOP opinion poll published by the *Journal du Dimanche* shows that public trust in the reform is low, almost two-thirds (64%) of people do not trust the system to be fairer.[6] Without public trust it seems impossible to imagine the proposal gaining consensus and reform, once again, will hit a wall.

Without Trust Potential can be Wasted

If businesses and citizens do not trust policymakers to continue to grow the economy and create an environment where these agents can reach their potential, then this can have catastrophic consequences. Business do not open new operations in countries where there is no trust in the rule of law or political leadership. The same logic can be applied to investment theory: businesses do not continue to invest in a society that they do not trust to be a safe place for investment and return. Trust in the economic system does not just impact business but also it impacts citizens. If citizens do not trust that they can accomplish their objectives or achieve their dreams in their own country, then they will consider alternatives which contributes heavily to brain drain, especially in developing nations. Research has investigated the occurrence of brain drain in China during the later years of the previous decade. Beginning in the 1970s, students from China were encouraged to study at universities abroad to benefit from western education but the plan was for those students to return to China after finishing their studies. It was expected that when they returned, they would bring with them a wealth of knowledge and new skills which would be used back in China – however it is suggested that only 5% of students returned. Zweig (1996) finds evidence to suggest that there was a lack of trust among these students in the political stability and economic landscape of the nation which lead to them remaining outside of China.[7]

The evidence on the benefits of collaboration between policymakers and citizens is endless. However, citizens are unlikely to engage in collaboration if they do not trust that their input will be considered. These concepts are intertwined: low levels of trust can contribute to insufficient collaboration and low levels of collaboration can contribute to a lack of trust. Therefore, trust is vital if policymakers want to **enhance levels of collaboration**. Evidence from the UK has shown that in order to progress with political change levels of trust in government need improving and greater collaboration is a clear route to achieving this.[8]

Policymakers and their staff spend considerable amounts of time focusing on how to best position policy changes. A powerful narrative is often said to be the key to success. However, without trust it does not matter how powerful the speech or narrative being portrayed, the policy will fall on deaf ears. **A powerful narrative can be enhanced through greater levels of trust.** For all the reasons above, and more, without trust policymakers will fail to enact change and they will not gain votes in an election, again highlighting the ability to proxy trust for political legitimacy.

The consequences of a lack of trust can be profound. Unfortunately, it is no mystery that **policymakers around the world are facing a legitimacy crisis**. In many circumstances, they continue to govern although they have lost the trust of their nation. In 2019, only 45% of citizens in OECD nations trusted their government.[9] Trust in government has been eroded since the 2008 Financial Crisis and continues to deteriorate in many parts of the globe. The UK has considerably low levels of trust in government compared to the countries in the European Union. In 2001, just 31% of the UK population stated that they trusted the national government, by 2019 this had fallen by ten percentage points to just 21%.[10] Alongside reported levels of trust in government there are a range of indicators which signal we are experiencing a legitimacy crisis.

In the 2016 US election, voter turnout was only 56%, which represents a slight uptick on the previous year but is considerably lower than the rate of the 2008 election.[11] This could signal a lack of trust in those nominated for election. The polarisation of politics across the globe could lead to high levels of inequality in trust among citizens. Growing distrust is particularly concerning in the context of the 'post-truth' era. The UK's vote to leave the European Union could also be construed as a legitimacy crisis between the EU and the British public, with UK citizens no longer trusting in the EU to operate in their best interest.

Legitimacy crises are often accompanied by an increase in protest movements. The recent developments in the United States are signals of a legitimacy crisis and also signal a considerable breakdown in trust between the police and several members of the public. This shows that worrying levels of distrust are not exclusive to governments but are occurring in other institutions including the police, the media and even among fellow citizens. However, across OECD countries trust in government is lower than trust in local police, education providers and healthcare professionals.[12] **The factors behind this decline in trust are various and connected,** including rising inequalities, higher citizen expectations, socio-economic crises and many more. However, the impact is the same and is a significant one. Levels of trust in institutions vary based on various factors including the individual's income, education, nation or political view. Therefore, rebuilding trust is not easy. There are some signs trust is recovering from its post-financial crisis low – although it is unclear what impact the current COVID-19 crisis will have on trust and legitimacy.

Trust can be related to an individual's dealing with government institutions but can also be based on the perception of how much impact government actions have on their own lives. The feeling that the system or government works to protect groups that do not include you can lead to a high level of distrust. If the government is no longer perceived to be successful in solving the social and economic problems of its citizens, then individuals will be convinced the government is failing them and hence it loses legitimacy in their eyes.[13]

Indeed, holding high levels of trust can be a strong accelerator for policymaking by reducing transaction costs, enhancing compliance, improving enforcement and strengthening the power of narratives. However, current evidence suggests trust is not at its optimum level and change needs to occur.

Performance-Based Legitimacy, Decentralisation and the Decrease of Trust Requirements

An interesting finding from our research is the expanding importance of performance-driven legitimacy. Statistically speaking, this is reflected in the low explanatory power of the legitimacy variable as proxied by trust in government on development performance when accounting for the performance-related variables of the Energy block such as the optimality of the policy mix and administrative efficiency. This aligns with our framework of civilisational ages (Figure 35). Granted that most policy systems in the world are currently operating under the 3rd age or transitioning to the 4th age, one can assume that 'optimising' and 'autonomy' are the two dominant directions of development systems. Under the optimising direction, the high focus on tangible performance goals, such as economic growth and competitiveness, means a higher orientation towards a performance-driven legitimacy system. Indeed, the optimising direction entails reliance on accomplishments of concrete goals, such as economic growth and job creation, and the ability and expertise to do so as a basis for rising legitimacy. This is partly linked to evidence-based policymaking and the spirit of 'what matters is what works'. When effectiveness is the paramount criteria to judge public policies, then the ability to choose and implement policies that work becomes a significant source of legitimacy for the policymaker.

Figure 35.   Evolution of trust requirements throughout civilisational ages

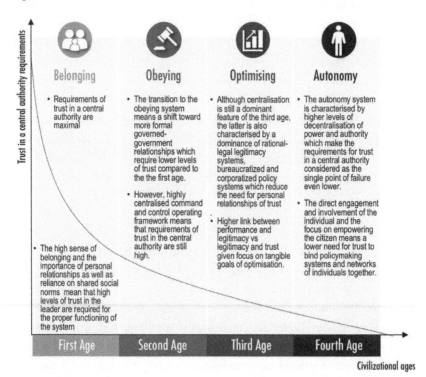

Source: Whiteshield

It also provides incentives for policymakers to optimise, claim to optimise, or claim the ability and expertise to optimise in order to gain further legitimacy. The optimising age relies on an impersonal, rational, bureaucratic and corporatist policy system following Weber's legal–rational type of legitimate rule which contrasts with personal authority relations based on trust. The transition to an autonomy age can also help explain the lower importance of trust in government. The autonomy system is characterised by high decentralisation which reduces the requirement for trust in a centralised authority such as the government. As mentioned previously, trust is a necessity in systems which are highly centralised. In countries or political systems where authority is centralised the government becomes the one point of failure. There is often a lack of citizen empowerment or engagement and therefore trust is needed to keep the system running. By contrast in decentralised systems, which enhance individual autonomy, the spread of authority across various actors progressively makes trust in centralised authorities effectively superfluous.

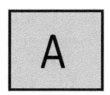

ADMINISTRATIVE EFFICIENCY: THE IMPORTANCE OF INSTITUTIONAL MEMORY AND THE ADMINISTRATIVE LEARNING CURVE

Administrative efficiency is the second energy multiplier. Choosing the right policy mix is one thing, implementing it correctly is another. For policies to be designed and implemented successfully the administration must have the necessary knowledge, memory, institutional structure and resources.

A   Administrative efficiency
• Administrative efficiency reflects the skills, capacity and resources of the administrative system which shape the quality of policy implementation and delivery. The level of administrative efficiency depends on the positioning along the learning curve.
• The administrative learning curve itself depends on a wide range of factors including organisational structures and knowledge management processes.
• Administrative efficiency can be quantified by using the complexity and sophistication of policies of a country as a proxy for its administrative capabilities.

Organisational Structure, Skills and Implementation Gaps

Inefficiencies arising from the implementation process are omnipresent and can be driven by a variety of factors from capabilities, skills, and a lack of knowledge to bureaucracy or corruption. In modern policymaking and implementation, a lack of digital skills in government and the public sector can prove highly consequential. For instance, if public sector staff fail to collect and analyse the right data this can lead to poorly designed policy that does not consider real-world indicators. A similar argument can be made against bureaucracy and departmental silos: policy does not occur in a vacuum and neither should policy design. For instance, implementing changes to education policy intended to improve employment in certain sectors is unlikely to have the desired outcome without consulting the department for labour or engaging external institutions.

Failing to address these inefficiencies leads to policy implementation gaps, that is the difference between what was planned and what occurs. The difference between expectation and reality can be realised in different ways: a policy can cause less change than expected, have unintended consequences, cause distress to those involved or cost more than anticipated. The extent of policy success can be plotted on a spectrum and at one end are policy failures. There is debate on what constitutes a policy failure. In reality, the larger the gap between reality and expectation, the more likely it is that the policy can be deemed a failure.

Administrative efficiency can also include how public administrations can better work together and how they can better engage with citizens to improve delivery of services or programme-specific refinements. Higher levels of administrative efficiency can be achieved when there is an organisational structure that includes outreach to citizens and other third parties.

In recent years, Australia has demonstrated innovation in its approach to citizen engagement in policymaking. Their method shifts engagement from acquiring buy-in to building ownership. In turn, this creates more legitimate solutions to the policy questions of the day. Dialogue and back and forth with citizens can create a greater sense of control than simply public voting or petition sites which have been used as engagement mechanisms in other countries. The Australian model includes engagement across government and reduces the impact of the silos. The increasingly complex and interconnected policy landscape needs innovation and learning which has been put at the heart of the Australian approach.[14]

Institutional Memory and the Administrative Learning Curve

A key factor to consider is the learning potential that failure brings. Various unexpected issues can arise in the implementation process of policies but what matters is activating the institutional memory and learning from those issues and mistakes to improve the implementation process in the following iterations. In public policy, very few ideas are new. They have either been tried before in the country in question or elsewhere. Government officials often come and go with election cycles or reshuffles, but the public sector workforce (civil service) is a vital resource. When public sector resources work effectively, their institutional memory should include how governments reacted to previous crises or periods of economic downturn. This can improve the agility of decision-making and result in more efficient policy implementation. Although, in practice, this does not always occur. Protecting national institutions against high levels of staff churn should hence form a core component of any plan to enhance the quality of policy implementation. The importance of learning from previous successes and failures holds true across the public and private sector. It is one of the reasons firms place such a high value on staff retention and internal promotion. Research conducted by Spencer Stuart into the CEO transitions of S&P 500 companies highlights the value of institutional memory. In 2019, only 21% of new CEOs were external hires.[15]

Active institutional memory allows administrations to move up along the administrative learning curve and decrease implementation costs through experimental learning (Figure 36).

Drivers of Institutional Memory and the Strength of the Administrative Learning Curve

This institutional memory and administrative learning curve are far from an automatic process. On the contrary, public administrations and policymakers are often accused of poor knowledge management or institutional memory loss.

Figure 36.   Modelised administrative learning curve

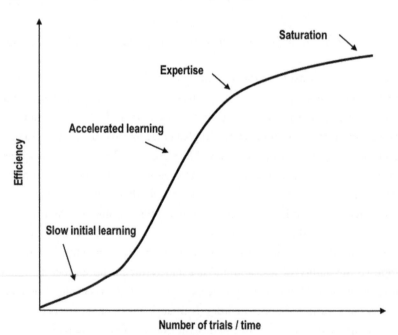

Source: Whiteshield Partners

In the case of France, a lack of institutional memory has been a major component of its inability to enact major labour market and pension reforms. In the mid-1990s, the French government tried to implement labour market reform to tackle youth unemployment. Contrat d'insertion profressionnelle (CIP) was a scheme that enabled young workers to be paid below the statutory minimum wage for up to two years. The aim was to encourage employers to recruit. Despite the well-meaning aim, the policy was not well received and triggered several weeks of protests. Eventually, the government had to scrap the policy, just one month after decree. This should have been a moment for institutional learning; however, these failings have been repeated in more recent attempts at reform including *El Khomri Law*, which was introduced in 2016, and attempted pension reforms in 2019.[16]

Several factors can strengthen administrative efficiency and the subsequent position on the administrative learning curve, including organisational structure, knowledge management and policy experimentation (Figure 37).

Organisational Structure

The organisational structure of administrations can also play a significant role in institutional learning. It has indeed been noted that centralised systems tend to suffer more from institutional amnesia compared to decentralised structures. Centralised agencies can lead to increased memory loss due to attracting highly skilled staff with a tendency of churning through the various departments and positions of decision-making which are in large supply in centralised governments. In contrast, decentralisation can lead to increased specialisation due to the value placed on institutional knowledge and less churn due to the short supply of alternative positions in similar policy sectors or local areas.

Finally, organisational structures also have tools to consciously accelerate the administrative learning curve through experimental practices. Experimental practice can include pilot schemes, behavioural based trials and virtual environments for policy or regulatory change. One country unexpectedly pioneering in this area is China. Policy experimentation is an effective mechanism to induce behavioural change, find out what works on the ground and produce institutional innovations that are conducive to investment, entrepreneurship and economic growth. Heilmann (2007) suggests the

Figure 37.   Drivers of differences in administrative learning curves

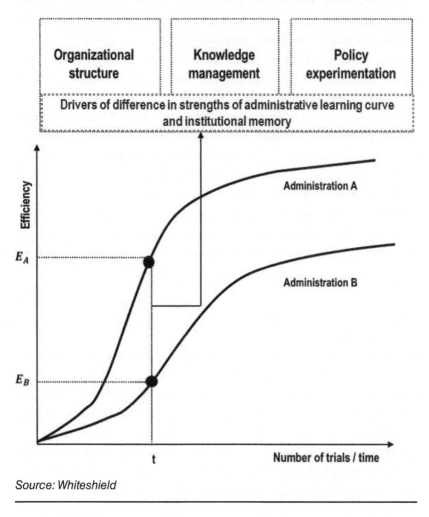

Source: Whiteshield

distinctive nature of Chinese policy experimentation has likely contributed to its economic rise.[17]

Knowledge management

Knowledge management is a core component of mitigating against poor administrative efficiency. Effective knowledge management structures should be incorporated into governments and institutions to create an environment conducive to internal knowledge sharing. Governments are less proficient in knowledge management capabilities compared to industry, which has understood the value of this intangible asset for years. Knowledge management can be essential in combatting the impact of churn on institutional memory and in enabling greater institutional learning.

Policy Experimentation

Policy experimentation and learning adoption is not as widespread in highly developed economies. In Europe, Finland is leading the way by moving to a speculative model of policymaking which is experimental, and evidence-based. In recent years, Finland has undertaken a policy experiment associated with the much-discussed area of Universal Basic Income. The UBI experiment involved 2,000 unemployed individuals aged 25–38 and lasted two years. The aim was to see whether UBI could be the solution to the changing economic environment.[18]

Moving up the administrative learning curve is not purely dependent on internal learning but on policy diffusion and the sharing of international best practice. Some countries are known to be innovators and others are emulators. Maggetti and Gilardi (2016) demonstrate three reasons as to why policy diffusion occurs. First, previous policy successes or failures can shape decisions to adopt similar ideas in other countries or states. Second, policies can be legitimised if they are valued highly by peers, which means policies are seen as the go-to response to a given problem. Finally, change can be attributed to the need to remain competitive compared to other countries. This is often the case with tax policy.[19] There is a tendency to focus on policy diffusions that have been successful without considering those that have failed and the causes of these failures. If policies from elsewhere are simply 'copied and pasted' to new countries without considering local conditions the implementation gap will be large and the policy is unlikely to achieve the desired outcomes.

A country that has avoided the failures of other countries is Norway. As oil production began in the 1970s, the country realised the opportunities and risks this brings. The paradox known as 'Dutch disease' means that countries reliant on a specific industry or natural resource often face economic decline in other areas. Norway understood the problems other oil-dependent countries faced and sought out ways to ensure sustainable management of petroleum assets and revenues, creating wealth and an economy that would thrive beyond oil production. This aim was achieved through the creation of a sovereign wealth fund, which is common practice in resource rich nations. However, to distinguish itself from other nations, Norway has used its wealth fund to create an investment portfolio.[20] The country spends the returns on investment rather than living off the value of assets themselves.

Efficiency Goes Beyond the Traditional Cost–Benefit Approach to Include Resilience Notions and Evaluation

An administration incapable of learning from its experience is bound to keep repeating past mistakes and be unprepared to face disruptions and systemic risk. South Korea was praised for its highly efficient response to the early stages of the COVID-19 pandemic, but it does not hold a perfect record in dealing with public health emergencies. In fact, various policy failures during the 2003 SARS outbreak, the 2009 H1N1 influenza pandemic and the 2015 MERS crisis all contributed to an incremental improvement of disaster risk management and public health emergency response mechanisms. This culminated in a clear comparative advantage when dealing with the COVID-19 crisis, one that is first and foremost driven by active institutional memory and a strong administrative learning curve.

There are parallels to be drawn outside of government, from the private sector. During times of change (or crisis) corporate memory is a core component of a firm's ability to absorb and adapt to change. Hence, corporate memory as a driver of corporate resilience, needs to remain both dynamic and continuous to truly allow best practice to continue to be adopted and enacted.

Unfortunately, politicians are inherently more likely to engage in short-termism due to the structure of the election cycle. To paraphrase American journalist Esther Dyson: 'in politics the dominant timeframe is a term of office, in fashion and culture it's a season, for corporations it's a quarter, on the internet it's minutes, and on the financial markets mere milliseconds'.[21] The biggest civilisations in history can serve as warning signs for what occurs when there is a failure to think long-term and tackle the big issues of the day. The Roman Empire, for example, engaged in a continuous debasement of its gold and silver coinage that contributed to its final collapse.[22]

The growth of behavioural science in recent years demonstrates the value put on evidence and evaluation in policy. There is knowledge to be gained in understanding how individuals react to change. Subsequently, this can enable policy tweaks and contribute to significant improvements in desired outcomes. Learning from past iterations, evidence and evaluation are core components on which to build the foundations for specific learning. In 2010, the UK announced plans to overhaul its welfare system through the introduction of Universal Credit (UC). Following a 2013 publication by the National Audit Office highlighting UCs multiple failings, steps were taken to improve policy learning and adjust the implementation of the programme. These included new leadership and a phased roll-out approach involving breaks so changes could be made based on real-world evidence.[23] This learning reduced the scale of failings and stopped the policy from being scrapped.

Changing policy based on evaluation and learning was harnessed by Mexican policymakers, through the scheme initially known as Oportunidades. This poverty reduction scheme provided mothers with money to encourage them to send their children to school and to the health centre. The programme included an impact assessment at the heart of its design. Assessment and learning allowed the scheme to be modified and adapted according to the context of each country that tried a similar scheme. Oportunidades changed during the years of use and before it was stopped it was known as Prospera. It was not just the name that changed: the programme had expanded to favour the social and productive inclusion of beneficiaries.[24]

POLICY NARRATIVE: THE POWER OF COMMUNICATIVE ACTION

When enacting specific instruments, policymakers are also constantly communicating a story, providing a meaning and identity to these instruments. This story is carefully constructed based on evidence and the principles of political discourse, rhetoric and persuasion.

N	Narrative

- The story or narrative created by policymakers is essential to the take up of policies. The importance of narratives shouldn't be undermined by following the logic that only actions matter in policy. An inconsistent, contradicting or weak narrative will not create the environment needed for a policy to succeed.

- The strength of a narrative depends on several factors including its outreach and the extent of its audience, its consistency with policy goals and policies, and its leveraging of the key values and beliefs of the community.

- The strength of the narrative can be quantified through metrics of policy communication (in terms of outreach) and discourse analysis methodologies (in terms of consistency and alignment).

The importance of these principles in public policy is not new and forms the basis of numerous academic studies and theoretical frameworks. A core component of this work is focused on the choice of words in political speeches to convey meaning and sentiment. Work by Chilton (2004) suggests that political discourse to demonstrate an ideological stance or identity goes beyond the choice of specific words to include aspects such as the way words are spoken, the choice of language, the accent used and the usage of imagery.[25]

The impact of official discourse might be disregarded following the principle that actions matter more than words. However, that would be undermining the idea that development is a story of change – partly of social change – and that individuals respond to shared values, symbols, beliefs and meaning. There is agreement among most social scientists, including Burstein (2016), that public opinion shapes policy, especially when an issue is of considerable importance.[26] The question of narrative is usually approached from this bottom-up perspective: how will public opinion shape policy discourse. Urging individuals to take into consideration the other side of the coin might be qualified, by some, as a neo-paternalistic perception of society, a critique often directed to behavioural policy.

Yet political discourse and narrative can have a significant impact on public opinion. Political discourse can be **persuasive and enact change**. Key speeches in history are said to have 'changed the world' through their ability to enact change. From Martin Luther King's 'I have a dream' to Winston Churchill's 'we shall fight them on the beaches', speeches can be powerful moments in history and lead to societal change. In the decades following Winston Churchill's speech, policymakers and politicians have tried to replicate his ability to create strong rhetoric during a time of crisis. George W. Bush is known for copying Churchill's style in the speeches he made following the events of the September 11th.[27] The usage of language and tone conveys images of strong leaders acting in the face of adversity. Vocabulary and tone can be utilised in different ways to call for action. For instance, both former presidents Barack Obama and Nicolas Sarkozy gave speeches at the UN's Climate Change Summit in 2009. Their choice of language demonstrates differences in their approach to persuasion. In his speech, Obama uses a dramatic narrative-based style that takes the audience on a journey towards the catastrophic events that could occur without change. He states that the US people are already on the path to change. In contrast, Sarkozy uses a more direct approach in his call to action and presents a pessimistic belief that we are on the wrong path to correcting climate change. However, his choice of language creates the image that he is the leader to correct this.[28]

Discourse can not only change the behaviour of the public but can also impact the **function of policymaking including through administrative efficiency**. Political leaders and ministers are not only running society, but they are also responsible for leading the public sector and consequently the civil service. Those critical of the government, including politicians and the media, can create an image of the public sector as overpaid, idle and members of the 'elite'. This dialogue can create an environment of low morale and disengagement within the public sector.[29] The Trump administration was a clear example of using dialogue against the public sector. State workers voiced their disagreement with several policies introduced by the administration and in return Sean Spicer (White House Press Secretary) delivered an ultimatum: they can 'either get with the program, or they can go', while President Trump himself has instigated rhetoric of public servants being disloyal and focused on their own agendas.[30] This can create divides between the public sector and the public based on their political persuasion. In the private sector the leadership style of CEOs and senior business figures is discussed as an important factor in motivating people and supporting the success of the business. However, similar comparisons are not drawn to the public sector irrespective of the fact that policymakers are as, if not more, important in shaping the opinions and actions of citizens and the public sector.

Discourse and rhetoric can be harnessed for the creation and moulding of social meaning and identity: they can impact our networks, our bonds with society and change levels of social cohesion. The direction of this change is dependent on the rhetoric deployed by politicians and the media. Attitudes to immigration and welfare recipients are a clear example of how narrative and rhetoric can influence the perception of an issue. Research produced by the London School of Economics has found evidence to suggest that the rhetoric and narrative used by politicians and the media has created a stigma around unemployment. Their research looked at the use of specific terms which aim at marginalising the unemployed including: 'something for nothing culture', 'life on the dole' and 'cycle of dependency'. These terms increased in usage throughout the period studied (1996–2016) and peaked in 2013.[31] They found a robust relationship between the negative framing of welfare recipients in national newspapers and tougher mindsets among citizens.

Once individuals have formed an opinion on a group of people, a policy or a political ideology, it is difficult to change their minds. When faced with facts that challenge an individual's world view, psychology suggests that they would simply rather deny the new evidence than change their opinion. Hence, public and political opinion is often formed by emotions and affiliations, not hard facts.[32] It is this inability to accept facts that are different to one's opinion that has paved the way for the 'post-truth' era. It is no longer about facts and evidence-based policy but about the rhetoric and discourse of those who share the same opinion.

In the context of societies around the globe that are facing increased polarisation, individuals can be highly influenced by the views and discourse of parties, leaders and policymakers. Polarisation is not exclusive to commonly discussed cases in the US and Europe – it is a global issue affecting countries including Turkey, Brazil and India to name a few. The 2018 election in Brazil was characterised by increasing levels of polarisation and a collapse of centre-ground politics. The outcome was the election of the right-wing ex-military officer Jair Bolsonaro over the left-wing candidate Fernando Haddad. During the election campaign there was discussion of 'dangerous levels of polarisation' and that the election would lead to the 'the end of democracy' in Brazil.[33] There is potential for damaging divisions to occur in almost all societies, even ones that seem fairly homogeneous. Research by Carothers and O'Donohue (2019) underscores the vulnerability of democracies across the globe to polarisation and the power of the rhetoric and discourse in fuelling the division.[34] There are steps national leaders can take to reduce levels of polarisation but first the leader must be willing, which seems unlikely in the most polarised countries.

In light of growing polarisation, studies of the influence of policy discourse on public opinion are gaining momentum. The present and recent past are not short of examples that demonstrate the influence of rhetoric and narrative. One of them is individual attitudes towards wearing masks during the COVID-19 pandemic, a subject which has become highly polarised in some countries such as the US. The narrative presented by leadership appears to be highly influential on individual and social beliefs. While health experts continued to suggest mask wearing would help to reduce the transmission of COVID-19, there was considerable pushback by groups of US citizens. During this time, President Trump was not helping to mitigate the polarisation of opinions, stating publicly in April 2020, in relation to mask wearing 'I don't think I'm going to be doing it.'[35] It was not until two months later, in July 2020, that the first image of Trump wearing a mask appeared, a clear change in message for the leader of the US.[36] Despite the rhetoric portrayed by the US media and on social media, self-reported mask usage in June 2020 was higher than other nations such as France, the UK and Canada. This suggests polarised opinions and narrative may gain attention but do not always represent the behaviour or actions of the many[37].

A powerful narrative is one that can nudge individual behaviour towards a desired direction aligned with development objectives. The question is: 'what makes a narrative powerful?' The answer is complex and based on multiple factors. The first factor is consistency: consistency of the narrative with actions and consistency of the narrative with development goals. Inconsistency or a 'do as I say not as I do' approach reduces the influence of discourse on public opinion and behaviour. Such behaviour leads to cognitive dissonance whereby an individual holds or demonstrates conflicting attitudes, beliefs or behaviours. Cognitive dissonance can be brought to life through the example of climate change: almost all citizens recognise it as fact and know that a reduction in emissions is needed. Nevertheless, we do not all drive electric vehicles, recycle to the extent needed or avoid international flights. Simply put, for many of us our behaviours contradict our beliefs. Policymakers should avoid inconsistencies in their messaging if they are to create powerful narratives and nudge public opinion.

The second factor is the outreach of the narrative or to what extent communication between policymakers and individuals is strong, frequent and sustained. Technological advances have increased the proximity between citizens and policymakers: from the fireside chats of Franklin D. Roosevelt to the instant tweeting of Donald Trump. In this age of social media, access to our leaders is one click away. Even five years ago in the US Facebook, was the most commonly cited source for news about government and politics among Millennials and Generation X.[38] This proximity could influence the power of government rhetoric. However, in fast news cycles and where misinformation can spread rapidly it can be hard to cut through and have a real impact on behaviour.

The third factor which impacts the power of narrative is the leveraging of common beliefs and values. Indeed, even if the narrative's purpose is to enhance change it should be grounded in the sociocultural context and the set of core beliefs at the heart of social identity and meaning. By leveraging these principles, we experience differentiated narratives on the same issue based on the leader and the audience they appeal to. During her time as Prime Minister of the UK, Theresa May tried to establish the Conservatives as the political party tackling the environmental issues by tying the ideology of conservatism with the need to tackle climate change. Throughout one her speeches she coupled the fundamental principles of conservatism with the need to build a better future and explicitly stated '...Conservatism and Conservation are natural allies.'[39] In contrast, Jacinda Arden's rhetoric on climate change is to position New Zealand as a pioneer of social change stating '... the question for all of us is what side of history will we choose to sit on' and making comparisons to historical changes such as nuclear disarmament.[40] The narrative creates the idea that there is no real choice on whether or not to act but that acting is a necessity. Political narrative does not just need to influence the public but also all interest parties and in the case of climate change this includes industry. Justin Trudeau's narrative in Canada has been dominated by tales of a win-win: the economy and the environment go hand in hand.[41] His sentiments have aimed to get business and industry on board with the mission to tackle climate change as persuading this group to take action is essential if real change is to occur.

Chapter Four

THE QUANTUM LEARNING

Individuals are not atomistic agents driven exclusively by the need to maximise their utility. We need to bring back the individual in its full complexity to the development formula.

The second building block of development is **quantum learning** or, as we define it, the ability of individuals to absorb public interventions and convert them into achievements and benefits.

More specifically, this ability translates into a spectrum of interactions between individuals and public policies ranging from awareness to comprehension, to adherence, and to compliance and, finally, conversion.

INDIVIDUAL MEANING

The ability of a person to absorb public policy and contribute to progress is determined by what we refer to as individual meaning.

- This relates to the abilities, aspirations, and motivations of individuals as conditioned by their backgrounds and their unique qualities.

- The backgrounds of individuals include economic, social and cultural capitals depicting, respectively, financial resources, strength of social network and relationships, and education and skills.

- The backgrounds of individuals include economic, social and cultural capitals depicting, respectively, financial resources, strength of social network and relationships, and education and skills.

The various dimensions shaping individual meaning can be grouped into three main aspects.

A first aspect can be linked to what the French sociologist Pierre Bourdieu calls the *'habitus'*, or the set of habits, skills and dispositions shaped by an individual's background which includes economic, social and cultural capitals. In more concrete terms these refer to material endowments, educational pathways, knowledge, intellect and intangible assets, strength and type of social network, and social relations. All of these factors impact an individual's ability to convert public policies in all fields. A recurrent example is education. Public provision of education and regulation of access through mandated years of compulsory education is the typical public intervention. Actual education outcomes will vary considerably from one society to another, from one individual to another and greatly depend on the absorption capacity. Financial resources, the educational background of parents, the social connections of families – all of these will determine if an individual will have access to education and what achievements and fulfilled opportunities this access can lead to.

Bourdieu's lifelong focus was how we interact sociologically and the factors which glue society together. It was through this work that his theory of society, which included habitus and capital, gained influence. Bourdieu stated habitus is: 'the dialectic of the internalisation of externality and the externalisation of internality or, more simply, of incorporation and objectification'.[42] Habitus can be summarised as the set of habits, skills and dispositions shaped by an individual's background which includes economic, social and cultural capitals.

Capital 1: Economic Capital

Economic capital denotes all types of material resources, including financial, property or land ownership, that could be used to an individual's advantage. In many aspects of life, it is still the case that the economic background of an individual matters a great deal in their individual achievements. The concept of social mobility causally links an individual's current economic capital to their future economic position. Across OECD nations, it would take someone born into a low-income family an average of four and a half generations to meet mean income in their society. Levels of social mobility vary by country, as does the importance of economic capital. In Colombia, it would take a low-income individual eleven generations to meet mean income. In comparison, it is only between two to three generations in Nordic countries.[43] Improving social mobility has been on the radar of governments for several years. However, tackling the importance of economic capital is difficult. Evidence from the UK shows that while government policy for the last two decades has tried to make strides in improving social mobility, little progress has been made.[44]

Levels of economic capital affect the absorption capacity of public policies. Across the globe the gap between the richest and the poorest is increasing, effectively the rich are getting richer while the poor get poorer. Since 1980, income inequality has grown rapidly in North America, China, India and Russia. Over the same time, inequality has grown moderately in Europe.[45] This rising level of inequality impacts the share of policy absorbed by high income individuals. The impact of your position on the income distribution scale and ability to absorb policy can be explained by examples including the role income plays in education attainment and completion rates. Across the OECD, there are disparities in educational attainment by economic background, with those from lower socio-economic backgrounds achieving lower PISA scores in reading, mathematics and science.[46] Education is not the only social indicator impacted by economic capital, another example is health. Even in countries with universal and free health services, such as the UK, economic capital or income influences health outcomes and life expectancy. In England, the gap in life expectancy at birth between the least and most deprived areas was 9.5 years for males and 7.5 years for females between 2016 and 2018; this represents an increase in inequality since 2013 to 2015.[47] Healthier and higher income individuals will be at an advantage when absorbing policies related to improving health and be in a better position to turn this into outcomes.

Therefore, potential policy absorption can be influenced by individual levels of income and wealth. The clearest example is tax. If changes occur to tax rates at the upper end of the income spectrum they will only impact those with income or wealth high enough to fall into those brackets. For example, in 2018, the US underwent significant reform to the tax system for individuals, however, there was no change in the tax rate payable for single individuals who earn less than US$9700 per annum.[48] The system overwhelmingly benefits those on higher incomes due to changing income thresholds and reductions in the tax rate. Those on low incomes cannot absorb the policy. Other examples include income-based compulsory benefit schemes, such as Superannuation in Australia and Automatic Enrolment in the UK. In these schemes, employers must pay into a pension for staff who earn above a salary threshold, therefore those on the lowest incomes are not able to benefit from the policy.

Capital 2: Cultural Capital

According to Bourdieu, **cultural capital** is the cultural knowledge that helps us navigate situations and alter our experiences and the opportunities available to us. Cultural capital can include education, style of speech (including accent), the way someone dresses and their level of intellect. There are numerous examples of how cultural capital can influence individual outcomes.

There has been considerable discussion among social scientists and policymakers around access to elite occupations and the hiring practices of those in top firms. It is often said that individuals hire people who are like them and often base this decision on cultural factors such as accent, dress sense and cultural references or knowledge. In these situations, cultural capital can be of extreme importance in the success of an individual in their job search and movement into high-paid occupations. In the UK, the importance of cultural capital has been recognised by the agency responsible for monitoring the standard of education institutions. The Office for Standards in Education (Ofsted) has included cultural capital into its monitoring of the quality of education. It defines cultural capital as 'the essential knowledge that children need to be educated citizens'.[49] Incorporating cultural capital into the curriculum could include initiatives such as more school trips to museums and foreign countries, and changes to the books stocked in the school library.

Various statistics highlight the role of cultural capital. For instance, the proportion of CEOs with degrees (and even specific subjects) and the income of those with degrees.

Bourdieu is known for applying the concept of cultural capital to educational attainment. There is a wealth of evidence on the impact of cultural capital on educational attainment and the mechanism through which the influence can occur, including the judgement of teachers based on a range of social indicators or the decision of parents to actively invest in their child's acquisition of cultural capital. One recent study has used sibling education data to study the causal effect of cultural capital on educational attainment. The study finds evidence of a significant causal relationship between the two factors.[50]

Specific examples of the key role of cultural capital, in both life achievements and policy absorption, are evident across a broad range of sectors, institutions and policy initiatives. The on-going accumulation of skills and knowledge throughout one's working life is an important tool to continue to move onwards and upwards in the labour market, especially as we continue to work later into our life. However, the accumulation of such knowledge and skill is linked to levels of social capital, including education. Across OECD nations, there is a clear correlation between formal and informal training participation and the level of education.[51] This could influence the ability of those with low levels of education to absorb public policies related to encouraging further provision of on-the-job training.

Beyond the implications in education and training there are other examples of cultural capital influencing policy absorption. It is important not to overlook the role cultural capital plays in many aspects of our life from our purchasing or consumption behaviour to our sense of humour. Changes to government policy on the subsidisation of cultural activities, such as museums, theatres or sports events, will be absorbed at differing levels based on the individual's level of cultural capital and the weight they put on certain activities.

Capital 3: Social Capital

The third and final concept is **social capital** which refers to the networks of relationships among individuals who live and work in society. Our network can be instrumental in helping us navigate life decisions and achieve our potential. There are three ways that social capital can have an impact: through the spreading of information, directly through influence and through social credentials.[52] The spreading of information is a key component of social capital. Hierarchical or well-positioned networks can alert individuals to opportunities that they would not have been aware of otherwise. Our networks can have a direct influence on our actions and outcomes, such as a hiring decision based on who you know or following your parent's occupation. The importance of social credentials may be less tangible but they are a core component of the social capital theory. They refer to the individual's ability to access resources due to their network, such as having someone 'put in a good word' or act as a reference in high-stake environments. This reflects the classic saying 'it is who you know not what you know'.

Social capital has an effect on outcomes. In the US education system, family ties to specific institutions can work in an applicant's favour when applying. Internships at major firms can be achieved through family ties and jobs

granted without a position ever being advertised for. These are just some of
the ways social capital can influence outcomes. A study of acceptance rates
into medical schools finds a significant increase in the probability of being
accepted to medical school in the US if your parents are doctors. This is significant even when controlling for acquired human capital and other factors.
Children of doctors are almost 14% more likely to be admitted into medical
school than comparable children of non-doctors.[53]

As with economic and cultural capital, social capital can influence policy
absorption. Policies focused on start-up growth or to encourage entrepreneurship will be absorbed at differing rates based on the social capital of
business owners. Those with the support of a network of individuals who
can help them navigate funding application processes or assist with business
plans will find themselves at an advantage in their ability to turn policy into
outcomes. These individuals can also use their social capital to secure additional funding through social credentials, find new ways to promote their
company or be aware of policies to support them in their journey through
shared knowledge.

In more concrete terms these three types of capital refer to material
endowments, educational pathways, knowledge, intellect and intangible
assets, strength and type of social network, and social relations. These factors do not operate in isolation but interact to impact an individual's ability
to absorb public policies in all fields.

Across economic, cultural, and social capital there were clear implications
for education. When nations seek to improve education outcomes across their
population, public provision of education and regulation of access through
mandated years of compulsory education are the typical policy interventions.
However, actual education outcomes will vary considerably from one society to another, from one individual to another, and greatly depend on the
absorption capacity. **It is clear that habitus impacts policy absorption.**

If we look in more detail at the impact of habitus on education policy
absorption it is apparent that those who benefit from prominent levels of
economic, social, and cultural capital are at an advantage, even in free education systems. Financial resources, the educational background of parents,
and the social connections of families – all of these will determine if an individual will have access to education and what achievements and fulfilled
opportunities this access can lead to. Bluntly, habitus will impact their ability
to absorb the policy of universal education.

Economic capital influences educational attainment through the type of school attended, the quality of teaching and the availability of learning resources. Across the world, differences in education outcomes are seen by socio-economic background.

Cultural capital includes education level and therefore can reflect the ability to move through the levels of education. It is unlikely for an individual to go onto tertiary education if they have not finished lower levels of education. The way someone dresses or speaks is also part of cultural capital and can influence the opinions of educators on the potential of children. Underestimating the potential of children could lead to reduced attainment. There is also engagement in cultural activities, such as sport and music, which can have an influence on educational attainment and the choice of institutions for further study.

Social capital is less tangible but reflects the networks of children during their time in education. Their parents and peers will influence their attainment. Parents are vital proponents of support and information during a child's formative years, including supporting with education tasks, providing information on vocational vs academic education, and the route to take. Evidence has also shown how our network of peers can influence education decisions and outcomes.[54]

The Dark Matter: the Inherent Specificity of Individuals

Finally, a third factor relates to an ***individual-specific quality***, one that cannot be directly measured or explained and that links to the inherent uniqueness of individuals, and to the heterogeneity and, to a certain extent, unpredictability of human pathways beyond determinants of background and sociocultural context.

THE COMMUNITY

A second factor can be referred to as the community or the set of informal institutions including norms, beliefs, traditions and symbols dominant in a society beyond the direct background of individuals.

C	Community

- The community represents the set of shared informal institutions which contribute to shaping individuals' beliefs, traditions or norms.

- The contribution of the community to the absorptive capacity of individuals depends on the alignment of those informal institutions, beliefs and values with the development vision of the policy system.

- The analysis of the community's contribution to quantum learning can rely on quantifying the alignment of community drivers with the development vision.

Social norms are the unwritten rules of how to behave in society which we follow, both knowingly and unknowingly. They can have a large influence on our beliefs and behaviours. The importance of these aspects is reinforced by the work of French sociologist Émile Durkheim who developed the concept of collective consciousness. The theory refers to the set of shared beliefs, ideas, attitudes and knowledge that are common to a social group or society (Figure 38). They inform our sense of belonging and identity, and our behaviour.[55] The concept signifies how unique individuals are bound together into collective units such as social groups and societies. Social norms can help us to explain the differences in the uptake of different activities across regions, states and between nations.[56]

The creation of social meaning or beliefs, norms and traditions can occur in a variety of settings. The general process of acquiring culture, adopting norms and developing an identity is known as 'socialisation'. First, there is primary socialisation which is the process whereby a child learns the norms, values and appropriate behaviours for an individual within society or the foundation of their community. Primary socialisation occurs predominately within the family unit, with learnings being passed on from parents, siblings or family friends. Much of our culture and identity is formed from our family, such as religion or diet – for instance, the child of vegetarian parents may grow up with the belief that it is not morally acceptable to consume meat.

Figure 38.   The three layers of the community grouped from most to least observable

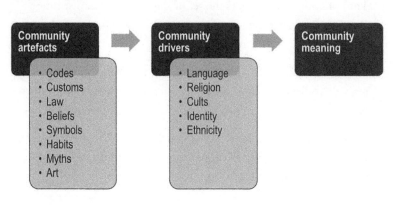

Source: Whiteshield

Secondary socialisation continues beyond the first few formative years of a person's life and includes learning how the behaviours are acceptable in smaller social units. It takes place outside the home and within institutions. Examples include learning how to behave at school compared to home or, in later life, learning the routines in a new job. Here we are moving beyond the background of individuals and habitus, and seek to understand how these informal institutions participate in shaping individuals' own beliefs and subsequently their interactions with public policies and the strength of the policy conversion factor.

There are various vectors which influence social norms including symbolism, the media and language. Language can be a strong mechanism for the transmission of social norms within cultures and across generations. The most explicit use of language in the transmission of information is through simple declarations which can alter individuals' opinions and beliefs: 'teachers are to be trusted' or 'it is wrong to lie'. However, language often conveys meaning in less explicit ways. Firstly, social identity through language variation, there are over 6000 languages across the globe, which are almost unintelligible to those who have not learnt them, with the learning occurring most often in childhood. Language and messaging can also alter our perceptions of groups of individuals, such as women as nurturing.[56]

While many social norms are adopted and entrenched in us when we are young, there are moments and mechanisms by which these social norms change. Our biases change our behaviours. Researchers have suggested that no one is bias-free, but some individuals let their biases influence their actions more than others, and these biases can evolve as the world around us changes. Social norms tell us that littering is unacceptable. However, evidence suggests that individuals are more likely to litter in areas where there is already rubbish, suggesting some degree of transiency in social norms.[57] Our norms can be altered by the actions of individuals or institutions with power. This is supported by a study focusing on attitudes towards same-sex marriage in the US before and after the Supreme Court decision that established it as a constitutional right. Surveys conducted before and after the judgement found that while personal opinions on same-sex marriage had not changed, individuals thought that their fellow citizens now supported same-sex marriage more than before, although in reality the only difference was the ruling of a public institution.[58] In the US, 72% of Americans say the state of moral values is getting worse in this country rather than better, despite many of the shifts being positive.[59] It is argued that to better understand behaviour change, there needs to be greater engagement with the links between shifts in social identity, and in-group norms.[60]

Impact of Social Norms on Quantum Learning

It is well documented in behavioural science, sociology and psychology that social norms can influence behaviour. The aim of a significant number of public policies is to promote or encourage the adoption of 'good' behaviour, such as volunteering or recycling, and reduce the incidence of 'bad' behaviour, such as littering or vandalism. The influence of social norms was once an overlooked area of public policies. However, the growth of behavioural economics, which seeks to bring the disciplines of psychology and economics together, has gained traction as a respected and much relied-upon discipline in recent years. A number of behavioural researchers have been awarded the Nobel Prize for Economic Sciences – including, in 2017, Richard Thaler who was awarded the Prize for his contributions to behavioural economics, most notably his work on nudge theory and rational choice.[61]

Scotland's Violence Reduction Unit has concentrated on turning social norms *against* gangs to tackle Glasgow's gang culture. Previous initiatives have only had short-term success. These methods included foot patrols and crackdowns on knife crime. Then Scotland's Violence Reduction Unit turned to a US programme called the Cincinnati Initiative to Reduce Violence (CIRV). A central plank of CIRV's approach is to make one gang member's actions affect all his/her peer group. So, if a gang member commits a murder, then the entire gang is targeted for offences: drug activities, weapon possession, and parole and probation violation. In other words, punishment is replicated in the same way as the delinquent behaviour was – through the social norm of gang membership. The use of similar schemes across the US have coincided with reductions in gang violence. These reductions have continued suggesting once a new social norm has been embedded, it becomes self-sustaining.[62]

There is evidence of using behavioural science and the influence of social norms to tackle the bigger issues of society, including corruption which still plagues much of the world. A behavioural study in South Africa has focused on how to alter social norms of corruption or bribery through the displaying of posters. Before, during and after placing posters throughout a medium-sized South African town, incentivised measures of social norms and bribery were assessed in a mobile lab. The descriptive norms poster, which included the message 'Less and less people from KwaZulu-Natal pay bribes' successfully changed incentivised social perceptions and individuals' willingness to engage in bribery in the subsequent game played for real money.[63]

Based on this evidence, it is therefore logical to investigate the impact social norms have on policy absorption. There are various examples that can illustrate this point. Many of those which come to mind will be policy issues where beliefs might have a greater role to play. It is easy to imagine how quantum conversion of redistributive taxation will vary greatly depending on sociocultural values such as individualism vs solidarity. There are a range of other factors which influence policy behaviours, such as beliefs on the role of each gender, climate change, religious beliefs or an appreciation for alternative medicine.

The interaction with environmental policies might be shaped by the prevalence of global warming scepticism, collectivism values and traditional relation to nature. To truly tackle the climate emergency, significant changes in behaviour will be needed which are dependent upon ensuring the public understand and *believe* the reality of the of the situation. A policy to increase the rate of recycling in a nation may be less effective if there is an underlying level of scepticism towards climate change, although the cost of the behaviour change is subtle, and therefore may not experience low levels of policy conversion. In contrast, halting international travel, installing new household energy equipment or buying an electric vehicle all require more effort from the individual – a policy to subsidise electric vehicles may be less effective among climate sceptics. A study in Australia found those who more strongly believed in human-induced climate change were more likely to support the mitigation scheme irrespective of its benefit and economic cost.[64]

In certain countries a tradition and belief in alternative forms of medicine or healing can be barriers to the uptake of more formal healthcare practices. Despite Uganda's success as a pioneer for AIDS prevention, an observational study in Uganda found that 1.2% of patients discontinued antiretroviral therapy (ART) which is used to halt the progression of HIV due to their belief that they no longer needed therapy because they had been spiritually healed.[65] Uganda is a highly religious country where 85.1% of the population identifies themselves as Christian and 12.1% as Muslim. The tradition of spiritual healing and religious belief is likely influencing the conversion of medicine availability policy into improved health outcomes.

In many cultures it is the social norm to wear a face mask when feeling unwell – in these countries the adoption of face masks in light of COVID-19 will have been easier. Some nations have had to mandate the usage of masks whereas in other countries the citizens have voluntarily increased mask usage.

The importance of social norms goes beyond the realm of common public policy problems to areas where we may not see the significance of social norms and beliefs. Innovation is a core component of business resilience in an ever-changing world. Evidence suggests innovative behaviours depend on norms and artefacts that support such behaviours, including an expectation from management that new ways of doing things should be tried.[66] However, there is no need to apply this only to businesses. The choices of a child as they move into adulthood are likely to be influenced by the external environment. The common saying 'you cannot be what you cannot see' is a clear example of how social norms can influence the path of certain groups in society – the United Nations has run a campaign on improving the representation of women in politics and parliament under this slogan.[67] Evidence from the US shows that exposure to innovation as a child can increase the likelihood of becoming an inventor. Growing up in an area or within a family with a high innovation rate leads to a higher probability of patenting in the same technology class as was common in the area. The relationship has a gendered element, with girls who grow up in an area with a high proportion of female inventors more likely to become an inventor in the same technology class.[68]

A less obvious but interesting example is the role of societal meaning in the first Industrial Revolution. Its flourishing in 18th century north-western Europe is often associated with a combination of factors including institutionalisation of private property, scientific discoveries and social values embodied in protestant religious beliefs. However, one dimension often overlooked is sociocultural attitudes towards merchants, traders and the 'bourgeoisie' in general. The American historian Deirdre N. McCloskey documents a strong shift in these attitudes, first in Holland, and soon afterwards in England, with talks of private property, commerce and innovation becoming far more approving and flying in the face of prejudices several millennia old. The wealth of nations, then, did not only grow so dramatically exclusively because of economic factors but also because rhetoric about markets and free enterprise became enthusiastic and encouraging around their inherent value.

Public Policy and Social Norms: Where do we Stand Today?

For too long, economics, which is a core component of public policy decision-making, has treated individuals as agents. One of the flawed aspects of traditional economics is the assumption of rationality, treating individuals as rational agents often ignores the complexity of belief systems and innate biases.

Indeed, most macroeconomic theories are micro-founded, that is they are grounded on an account of what typical agents do and why they do it. Macroeconomic aggregates (such as GDP, unemployment) result from the decisions of the millions of individuals populating the economy. Thus, it seems quite reasonable to study the dynamics of those aggregates by starting with the behaviour of single agents at the microeconomic level. Another crucial factor which justifies the use of micro-foundations in macroeconomics is the design of policies grounded in macroeconomic models that are not derived from first principles at the micro-level. Without the inclusion of micro-foundations these can be seriously flawed. This is because the reaction of agents to a given policy (e.g. lowering taxes) will change the parameters of the model used, when the effects of the same policy were estimated. Thus, without an understanding of such reactions, the desired results of a policy intervention can be invalidated.

Several of the assumptions used by traditional economic models or theories have been invalidated by several real-world cases. Economic models have an inability to model agents' behaviour. A recent example is the 2008 Financial Crisis which triggered a questioning of traditional methods and models. The remaining question is that of the alternative: how to account for agents' interactions, behaviour and choices if not through the traditional assumptions of economics.

There is a need for more accurate assumptions building on insights from other disciplines including but not restricted to cognitive and experimental psychology. Examples of these psychology insights already used in behavioural economics and behavioural policy are numerous, including prospect theory, bounded rationality, mental accounting and cognitive shortcuts. Evidently, the type of insight and disciplinary knowledge to mobilise differs depending on the nature of the policy issue to address and is not to be confined to psychological insights exclusively.

At the centre of behavioural economics is an assumption that it is more 'realistic' than neoclassical economics. However, some behavioural economic studies or pilots can overlook the inclusion of alternative thinking and other disciplines which could prove instrumental in truly understanding behaviours. By sticking with traditional methods of behaviour economics or policy, there is a risk that the importance of beliefs, social norms and tradition is ignored. Hence, bringing a new flaw to a discipline which was created to mitigate flaws and increase the inclusion of alternative disciplines within economics. Thus, while psychological and cognitive insights are without a doubt fundamental in advancing the adequacy of economic and policy models with the complexity of sociotechnical systems, there is no reason to exclude insights from other disciplines such as sociology or ethnology or to confine the social insights in these models to purely contextual influences in the decision-making process.

Agent-based models (ABMs) have gained traction as one of the solutions to addressing the flaws in how the behaviour of individuals is modelled. An ABM is a computational model which explores systems of multiple interacting agents or individuals which are spatially situated and evolve over the time. ABMs are highly effective in explaining how complex patterns emerge from micro-level rules over a period of time. ABMs explicitly recognise that the heterogeneity of agents and the behaviour and interactions between agents are conditioned not only by a set of behavioural rules which can directly incorporate the insights from cognitive and psychological experiments, but also from other social sciences such as sociology and anthropology.

QUANTUM LEARNING IN PRACTICE

The clearest example that brings this concept to fruition is the notion of non-take-up in welfare policies. Coverage of welfare policies is not the only defining factor of whether someone receives such benefits. They must have knowledge of their eligibility and choose to act upon this. Many welfare benefits require means testing and subsequently applying to receive payments. However, not everyone is aware of their eligibility, and some make an active decision not to apply for benefits.

Initially, non-take-up as a concept was applied to those specifically able to receive financial welfare payment but who did not receive them. The earliest definition for non-take-up was 'all persons or households entitled to receive financial social benefits who are unaware of their entitlement'.[69] The specific definition of non-takeup varies from country to country and in different studies. Non-take-up has been considered in various forms dating back to the public money crisis in England in the 1930s which discussed universal benefits vs targeting of social assistance.[70]

Measuring levels of non-take-up can be difficult and therefore the evidence base is thin and often outdated. The difficult part of estimating non-take-up is identifying the size of the population that is eligible. Household survey data can be used to estimate the gaps in provision of benefits and therefore non-take-up, although these sources still suffer from data challenges. OECD research suggests that across many European countries and welfare programmes the level of non-take-up ranges between 20–40%.[71] In the UK, where the concept of non-take-up is said to originate, an annual estimation of non-take-up of income-related benefits is produced. In 2017–18, it was estimated that six in ten of those entitled to pension credit took up the benefit, eight in ten of those entitled to housing benefit and nine in ten of those entitled to income support.[72] The rate of non-take-up is higher in Germany. Research by Harnisch (2019) suggests that between 2005–14 the level of non-take-up of unemployment welfare benefits in Germany was 55.7%.[73]

Understanding the scale and motivations for non-take-up are of considerable importance for policymakers. There are a number of disadvantages of non-take-up including ineffective public spending, a disconnect between intended and actual outcomes of a policy, and resource inefficiency. Another consequence on non-take-up of social welfare is that the policy is unlikely to achieve its goal of poverty reduction among the eligible groups or households. Given many of those eligible for social welfare benefits will be the most vulnerable in society, failing to reach all eligible individuals could lead to inadequate outcomes. There is also the impact that a lack of evidence on non-take-up, or the number of people eligible for a specific benefit, can have on forecasting the cost of the programme or the cost of reform. Policies which do not achieve the forecasted benefits through non-take-up could fail the government's own cost–benefit analysis assessments. Certain benefits can be used as identifiers for other state support and therefore the negative impact of non-take-up of one benefit could be compounding.

Given the significant financial and social costs of non-take-up it is imperative to understand why those eligible are not receiving the benefits to address these issues. Simplistically, we can divide the reasons of non-take-up into two groups: voluntary and involuntary. In the voluntary situation an individual or household knows they are eligible to receive social welfare but makes a choice not to apply or receive payments. Means-tested benefits can require complex and onerous application processes which can deter individuals from applying for support if they do not believe the benefits on offer are enough to warrant the difficult process. There can also be physical barriers to navigating the process such as a lack of digital skills for online applications or travel issues if claims must be made in person. Changes to eligibility or entitlement conditions can add further complexities which can alter the opinions and behaviours of potential claimants, such as persuading some to stop claiming, and thus contributing to voluntary non-take-up. There can be a harmful stigma around social benefits, or at least the perception of a stigma, which can deter individuals from claiming their entitlement. This is particularly likely to be true where there are conditions put on those claiming benefits or where there is a lack of trust in government institutions. Involuntary non-take-up is most common where the individual does not have knowledge of the welfare system and subsequently is not aware of their eligibility for support.

Non-take-up as a concept can be broadened. While non-take-up is primarily associated with social welfare benefits there are parallels to be drawn with other areas of government policy. Individuals choosing not to receive a benefit does not necessarily mean they are turning down financial gain. For instance, in a large number of countries free education is offered to young children and yet for various reasons not all children are enrolled in education. This can be construed as non-take-up: the benefit of education is on offer and yet some choose not to take advantage of this offering. In the UK, research has been conducted on the barriers to take-up of business support. It highlights the heterogeneity of the business community and the need for flexibility when designing the benefits of support programmes.[74] From vaccinations to microcredit there are many examples of non-take-up across the policy landscape, even those which appear to be more 'macro' and less directly impacting individuals' lives. For instance, a free trade agreement (which removes sectorial entry barriers) and other forms of high-level policy, still have elements of non-take-up. From one country to another the number of individuals able to achieve something due to a free trade agreement varies greatly.

The broadening of the concept is not just about applying it to other areas of policy but also about looking at non-take-up as a broad spectrum of possible interactions. It is not simply a binary decision of take-up vs non-take-up. Among those who do not take up a particular benefit there are different levels of knowledge, understanding and agreement which impact outcomes and have different policy implications. Take-up also occurs across a spectrum of possible outcomes including full take-up translating into the expected outcomes or take-up but with differing outcomes across participants or claimants.

Each position on the spectrum of take-up deserves an in-depth investigation.

To claim or act upon government policy initiatives the individuals or businesses must be aware of them. **Awareness or knowledge about public policy is an essential component of uptake.** There will be groups who are unaware of public policies which will in turn impact their ability to claim or act. Drivers of a lack of awareness or knowledge include language barriers, disengagement in public policy, education levels and social connections. A lack of knowledge is a prominent feature of welfare non-take-up.

Research conducted into non-take-up of the French minimum income (RSA) explicitly asks individuals why they did not apply for the scheme. The most common reason was a lack of knowledge with 68% of respondents reporting this reason, the next most common reason was a lack of need. Similar research in the Netherlands looked at the proportion of those who did not claim specific benefits due to an unawareness of the programme.[75]

Knowledge of a programme is one thing but understanding it is another. Individuals cannot be expected to claim or apply to receive benefits or support if they do not understand the specifics of the programme. Understanding of eligibility, associated benefits and conditions is crucial if someone is to take the time to apply. Means-tested welfare systems often come with complex processes and these can be barriers to understanding. For example, complex application processes may deter individuals from applying or multipronged means tests could lead some to believe they are not eligible when in fact they are. Those 'new to need' have been identified as at risk of non-take-up and could be deterred by a lack of understanding of all aspects of welfare support.

Local programmes have been used to improve the dissemination of information to the groups impacted by changes to welfare systems or new government programmes. These can prove essential in breaking through to the groups who are slightly removed from mainstream society. In the case of Slovakia, field social work (FSW) is a project whereby social workers help marginalised communities, mainly Roma, to integrate. While the direct aim of this programme is not to increase take-up of welfare benefits, evidence suggests that it has an impact on take-up.[76] These types of programmes can improve understanding of eligibility criteria and provide information to help navigate the steps required in order to make a successful welfare claim.

The spectrum of take-up is also influenced by the level of adherence or compliance. Individuals can have the correct level of knowledge and understanding but without compliance with regulations or policies non-take-up will still occur. Many cases associated with non-take-up highlight the importance of implementation alongside ideas. Beliefs, either personal, background-driven or societal, can play an important role in defining whether someone will adhere to government policy.

An example outside of the welfare system is that of tax avoidance. Individuals may know and understand their obligation to pay taxes but choose simply to not adhere to these regulations. Reasons for failing to comply vary by society and individual or business. However, regardless of the reasons why, a choice is still being made. In some instances, a lack of knowledge could be contributing to the 'non-takeup of tax compliance', however, it is unlikely in all circumstances. A study of factors influencing tax compliance in Kenya, South Africa, Tanzania and Uganda found that individuals who were more satisfied with the state of public service provision were more likely to support the government's right to taxation, thus supporting elements of the fiscal exchange theory. However, in this research the strength of the opinion varied based on the government's policy spending priorities.[77] Hence, in this case, their personal belief informs their non-take-up behaviour.

There are numerous additional drivers of non-compliance including stigma, skills, tradition or inertia. In Italy, reform to the social care sector occurred in 2012 through the Home Care Premium. In summary the programme was a cash-for-care scheme designed to cover the costs of employing an at home care assistant. Evidence supported the design and implementation of the programme, however, success was thwarted by high levels of non-take-up. It was not a lack of knowledge or understanding that resulted in the high levels of non-take-up but individual decision-making on the cost vs benefit of applying and the associated stigma of receiving funds.[78] In this scenario, societal opinions and the role of tradition are key drivers of non-take-up.

Non-take-up due to beliefs, either personal or societal, can occur in response to environmental policies. Research has found that cultural factors influence how firms behave, including with respect to the environment and innovation. Analysis of 591 corporations found that a firm's environmental performance is influenced by the culture characterising the country where the headquarters are based.[79] Therefore, we can infer that the take-up of environmentally friendly positions is dependent on the beliefs of the population.

Take-up is not limited to adherence but is also conditional on the converting of policy into achievements. Alongside the traditional drivers of non-take-up explored above there is an unknown or 'dark matter' that remains specific to the individual and is not conditioned by their background or society.

Evidence from the implementation of microfinance schemes in different countries demonstrates how outcomes are not always as expected. A study focused on microcredit in Hyderabad (India) found that although take-up of microcredit occurred and outcomes were achieved in relation to small business investment and profit, no change was observed in consumption. There were also no significant changes in health, education, or women's empowerment.[80]

Regardless of take-up, differences in achievements can occur. For instance, even when there is almost full compliance and take-up of free and universal

education, it is well documented that not all individuals gain the same achievements. Hence, universal access to education does not translate into universal
outcomes. Even in the most developed countries, where actions have been
taken to standardise the quality of teaching across education establishments
and education attendance is compulsory, education-based outcomes are still
highly correlated with an individual's social background. In this scenario, an
individual's characteristics influence their ability to 'take-up' the expected
benefits.

Differential achievements are common in all areas of policy, especially
when they rely on individual decision-making or characteristics. Research on
microfinance shows that while most microfinance investments are profitable
there is considerable heterogeneity in profits.[81] This type of heterogeneity in
outcomes associated with the take-up of microfinance can inevitably cause
non-take-up among other groups. This is because it can contribute to their
beliefs about the system as potentially harmful or not worth the required
effort.

Non-take-up clearly falls across a spectrum of possible interactions with
a complete lack of knowledge at one end and differences in achievement at
the other. However, there is no systematic study of the factors that allow
individuals to achieve more from public policies. There is a heavy reliance on
randomised control trials (RCTs) as the gold standard where the purpose is
to have random sampling in order to evaluate the impact of policies indepen-
dently from beneficiaries' characteristics and so to neutralise the influence of
individual variables. However, we can see throughout the policy landscape,
from tax avoidance to education outcomes, individual characteristics matter.

Chapter Five

QUANTUM GOVERNANCE IN PRACTICE

The objective is not to provide policymakers with new knowledge but rather to provide them with a new public policy code, a knowledge regime and the cognitive infrastructure needed to translate a theoretical framework into actionable strategies.

In the previous chapters we introduced the quantum equation of development, a framework to understand and track the drivers of development and analysed its components grouped into two main blocks: the Energy block and the Quantum Learning block.

However, the objective of any theoretical framework is ultimately to guide action, to align the practice with the conceptual foundations. In this last chapter we introduce a five-phase methodology showcasing how to use the quantum governance framework in real-world public policy settings.

The five phases of the guide (Figure 39) are: 1. Identifying the 'rules of the game'; 2. Setting the theoretical foundations; 3. Establishing a strategy; 4. Outlining a plan; 5. Implementing the plan.

Figure 39. Five steps of the quantum governance toolkit

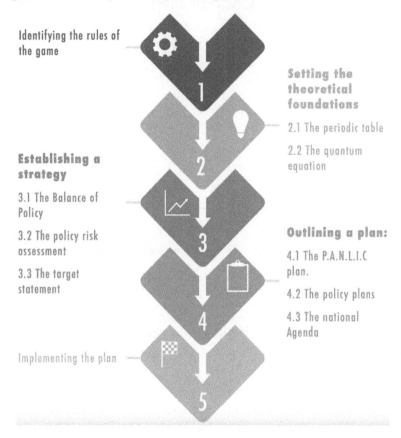

Identifying the rules of the game

Setting the theoretical foundations

2.1 The periodic table

2.2 The quantum equation

Establishing a strategy

3.1 The Balance of Policy

3.2 The policy risk assessment

3.3 The target statement

Outlining a plan:

4.1 The P.A.N.L.I.C plan.

4.2 The policy plans

4.3 The national Agenda

Implementing the plan

Source: Whiteshield

1. IDENTIFYING THE 'RULES OF THE GAME'

Nowadays, very few public policy meetings will start by discussing foundational questions such as: 'in which system are we operating?' and 'in which system do we want to operate?'. That is because we usually take the answer for granted. We think of it as an immutable external constraint imposed by a global world order.

We imagine a change in the system as something so drastic and consequential that it cannot go unnoticed and thus the 'rules of the game' for this system do not require periodic questioning. Yet History tells us that foundational changes in societal or civilisational frameworks do not happen overnight. They are long processes involving complex interactions and hidden dynamics, which can be well under way and even completed before talks about a paradigm change start.

Understanding the broader paradigm under which policy systems are operating is critical to identify the constraints and operating rules of the framework. Based on our four ages of development presented in Chapter 1, we have identified a set of questions that policymakers can start with to derive the 'rules of the game' (Figure 40).

1. What is the direction? The point here is to identify the broader objective that guides every action in social organisation. To illustrate this, for several decades that direction was 'optimising'. There was strong pursuit of economic growth by countries, a profit maximisation mindset in firms, and a prioritisation and valorisation of efficiency for people – doing more with less rose as a common mantra for all social organisations.

2. Who provides the voice of guidance? Who has the power to steer the ship? Whose advice is sought and trusted as a general truth? Under the 'optimise' system, that role was played by the 'economist'. The question needs to be understood metaphorically. This does not mean every head of state or every

Figure 40. Six questions for policymakers to identify the 'rules of the game'

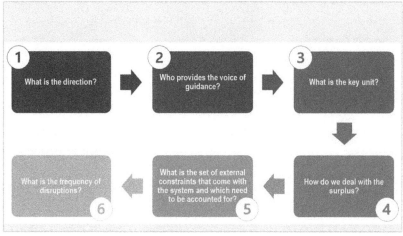

Source: Whiteshield

head of a company was an economist. It means that the cognitive infra-structure behind decision-making processes was dominated by the economists' knowledge regime. It means the institutionalisation of a set of tools, methodologies, types of reasoning, causal stories and assumptions from the realm of economics, and their use in virtually all areas of decision-making.

3. What is the key unit? The idea here is to identify the key element of action, the one targeted by every discussion of change, by every policymaking decision. That key unit used to be countries. It then progressively narrowed down to markets, firms, or sectors. Moving forwards, we argue that this unit should be the individual.

4. How do we deal with the surplus? Every society produces tangible resources and that production comes with a surplus. The idea is to understand who gets the surplus and how. Under the 'optimise' system, the mantra was to compete for the surplus. The surplus goes to those best at doing more with less.

5. What is the set of external constraints that come with the system and which need to be accounted for? Economic cycles are a typical example here. Countries, firms, and individuals know they need to deal with the consequences of growth and recession cycles that go beyond their power.

6. What is the frequency of disruptions? How frequently are societies hit by significant disruptions threatening their operating framework? Here, the historical pattern was the transition from low-frequency systems to high-frequency ones, where the disruption is supposed to come every decade or so.

These are the key questions that can be asked in order to derive the rules of the operating framework. These are, as explained, conditioned by the type of dominant system. In addition to them, however, there are the 'rules of the game' questions, parameters that countries can and need to set themselves.

1. What is the 'north'? What are the development goals to achieve? What model of society is aspired to?

2. The time horizon: What is the priority timeline for the development path given potential trade-offs between different time horizons and different types of actions?

2. SETTING THE THEORETICAL FOUNDATIONS

The 'rules of the game' have been identified, and the 'north' is set. Where do we go from here?

Say, for instance, that your country or society aspires to be inclusive and sustainable and that Sustainable Development Goals (SDGs) are considered the desired direction of development. How do you assess what policies are needed, and which ones need to be prioritised? The classic approach would be to go about this by dividing the development objective into a set of smaller ones related to specific policy domains: for example, increasing the quality of education or improving the business environment. Each smaller objective would be associated with a set of public policies from the same policy domain: for example, we need to increase public spending in education, or we need to hire more teachers. This falls under the 'silo' approach and is problematic because, in reality, development goals cannot be separated into smaller independent ones. Synergies and trade-offs arise continuously between them and a holistic approach is needed to assess public policies.

2.1 The Periodic Table of Public Policies

This is where we introduce our concept of a periodic table of public policies. What we need is a classification of public policies that does not simply follow the classification of abstract fields or silos but can give us insights on the patterns of impact associated with each policy. In the periodic table of elements, the classification of groups and families is based on shared properties between elements. Those properties indicate how the elements will 'behave' in a reaction. Effectively, what we are doing with public policies in the real world is no different to a chemical reaction: we are mixing different policies to achieve a certain objective and we need to understand how policies are expected to 'behave' in this mix. As mentioned in Chapter 3, we conducted this exercise for the case where SDGs are the development objective. Our starting point was a network of SDG outcome indicators coupled with a wide range of public policy indicators. Studying the linkages between policies and outcomes led to our periodic table (Figure 41). Each cell in the table is a public policy and the classification of groups, periods and blocks translates information about patterns of linkages for each policy. The groups

Figure 41. The periodic table of public policies

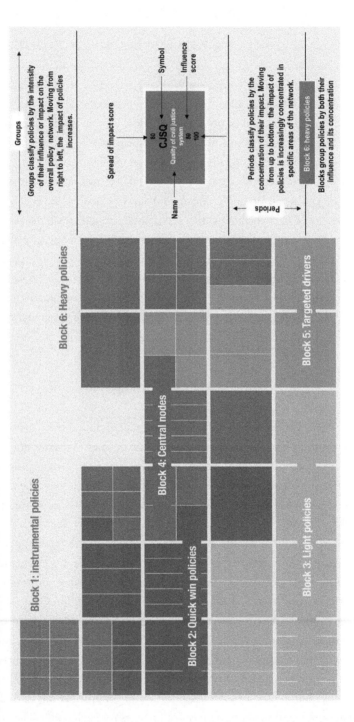

classify policies by the intensity of their impact while the periods classify them according to the spread of the impact across the network of policies and outcomes.

Guided by a periodic table of policies, can we move on to the strategy to adopt? No, this is where our quantum equation of development comes in. It is not just about policies and formal institutions; development drivers are much broader than that. The policy mix is simply one variable in the equation.

2.2 The Quantum Equation of Development

The quantum equation of development says:

$$D = E(P.L.A.N) \times Q(I.C)$$

Development performance (D) is function of Energy (E) and Quantum Learning (Q). The Energy input is itself a function of a society or country's policy mix (P), its legitimacy (L), its administrative efficiency (A) and its narrative (N). The Quantum Learning input is a function of individual meaning (I) which relates to the abilities, aspirations and motivations of individuals as conditioned by their background and their unique quality, and community (C) which includes the core values, beliefs and norms common to the individuals of a community as part of the collective consciousness.

Setting the 'D' or development performance parameter as SDGs and testing the equation in practice revealed that there are three paths to development. Firstly, there is an energy path, where development is led by the Energy block and where the quantum learning, or ability of individuals to convert policies into achievements, is lower than the energy introduced. Secondly, there is an individual-led path where quantum learning is higher than the policymaking Energy block. And thirdly, there is a quantum empowerment path striking the right balance between the two (Figure 42). Countries in the energy path face efficiency tensions where they are not improving in their development goals as much as they could, given the level of energy invested, while countries in the individual-led path face potential social tensions given that individuals can absorb and expect more energy than what is currently invested.

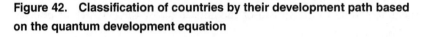

Figure 42.   Classification of countries by their development path based on the quantum development equation

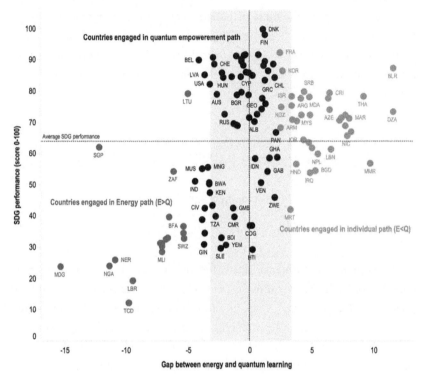

Source: Whiteshield

These are the main conceptual foundations to have before moving to the third phase: establishing a strategy.

3. ESTABLISHING A STRATEGY

At this stage you should be aware of the 'rules of the game', you should have set your development 'north' or direction, you should know that policies are only one variable in the equation of development, that your narrative, administrative efficiency and legitimacy matter for the energy derived from your policy mix, and that the ability of individuals to convert this energy into tangible achievements is the other side of the coin. Going from here, how do you set a development strategy?

3.1 The Balance of Policy

If you had just joined the strategy department of a corporation you would be handed a set of financial statements and looking at the balance sheet of the company will be your first step. What statements can you look at for a country? Well, there is the balance of payments, the BoP, but what does the balance of payments tell you? It is a record of all your trade and financial transactions. These are certainly important, but development is broader than product and financial transactions. This is why we suggest starting with a new BoP, the Balance of Policy (Figure 43). The Balance of Policy is a statement that summarises your inputs and outputs. The left entry gives policy outputs. This is simply how you perform in your set of development goals. In the context of SDGs, this entry would give you the distance remaining to achieve your SDGs. The right entry gives the inputs, and these are the variables identified on the right side of the development equation: your energy (and its subcomponents) and your quantum learning (and its subcomponents). The left and right entries need to balance out. Ultimately, they lead to the same number, following the logic that 'nothing is created, nothing is destroyed, everything is transformed'. There is no output that can emerge without a transformed energy or quantum learning input.

3.2 The Policy Risk Assessment

Once you have your Balance of Policy, and before deciding where you want to go from there, you need to assess your risks. Are you spending too much energy for the performance you are achieving? Are you spending not enough energy and might face social tensions? This would be the equivalent of knowing whether a company is in a deficit or surplus situation. For that your need the equivalent of a profit and loss statement (P&L). The development P&L outlines the gap between the potential development performance you could be achieving given your invested level of energy and your actual development performance (Figure 44). A positive development gap indicates a surplus: you are performing better than expected, while a negative gap indicates that you are performing worse than expected.

Figure 43. Illustrative Balance of Policy

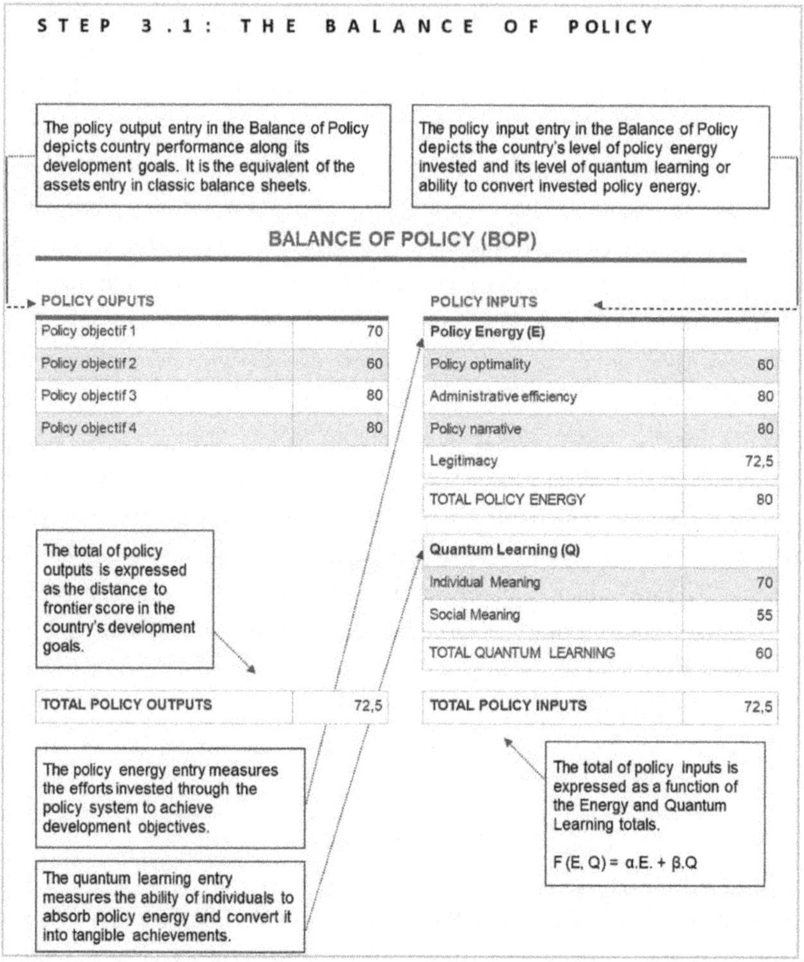

STEP 3.1: THE BALANCE OF POLICY

The policy output entry in the Balance of Policy depicts country performance along its development goals. It is the equivalent of the assets entry in classic balance sheets.	The policy input entry in the Balance of Policy depicts the country's level of policy energy invested and its level of quantum learning or ability to convert invested policy energy.

BALANCE OF POLICY (BOP)

POLICY OUPUTS		POLICY INPUTS	
Policy objectif 1	70	Policy Energy (E)	
Policy objectif 2	60	Policy optimality	60
Policy objectif 3	80	Administrative efficiency	80
Policy objectif 4	80	Policy narrative	80
		Legitimacy	72,5
		TOTAL POLICY ENERGY	80
		Quantum Learning (Q)	
		Individual Meaning	70
		Social Meaning	55
		TOTAL QUANTUM LEARNING	60
TOTAL POLICY OUTPUTS	72,5	TOTAL POLICY INPUTS	72,5

The total of policy outputs is expressed as the distance to frontier score in the country's development goals.

The policy energy entry measures the efforts invested through the policy system to achieve development objectives.

The quantum learning entry measures the ability of individuals to absorb policy energy and convert it into tangible achievements.

The total of policy inputs is expressed as a function of the Energy and Quantum Learning totals.

$$F(E, Q) = \alpha.E. + \beta.Q$$

In order to understand why you are in surplus or deficit you need an Energy–Quantum Learning (E–Q) P&L. This outlines the gap between the invested energy of the policy system and the ability of individuals to absorb and convert this energy. A positive E–Q gap indicates a surplus in energy: the introduced energy is more than individuals can absorb and convert, while a negative E–Q gap indicates a deficit in energy.

Figure 44.   Illustrative policy risk assessment

POLICY GAP		
THE DEVELOPMENT P/L		**THE E/Q P/L**

REALISED DEVELOPMENT PERFORMANCE (RD)		POLICY ENERGY (E)	
Policy objectif 1	70	Policy optimality	60
Policy objectif 2	60	Administrative efficiency	80
Policy objectif 3	80	Policy narrative	80
REALISED DEVELOPMENT PERFORMANCE	70	Legitimacy	72,5
POTENTIAL DEVELOPMENT PERFORMANCE (PD)		TOTAL POLICY ENERGY	70
Policy objectif 1	70	**QUANTUM LEARNING (Q)**	
Policy objectif 2	60	Individual Meaning	70
Policy objectif 3	80	Social Meaning	55
POTENTIAL DEVELOPMENT PERFORMANCE	80	TOTAL QUANTUM LEARNING	60
DEVELOPMENT GAP (RD-PD)	-10	**E/Q GAP (E-Q)**	10

- The development P/L outlines the gap between the potential development performance of the country and its realised performance: the development gap.
- The potential development performance captures the expected performance of a country given the level of policy energy.
- A positive development gap indicates a surplus in performance: the country performing lower than expected. A negative development gap indicates a deficit in performance.

- The E/Q P/L outlines the gap between the invested energy of the policy system and the ability of individuals to absorb and convert this energy.
- A positive E/Q gap indicates a surplus in energy: the level of policy energy is higher than quantum learning.
- A negative E/Q gap indicates a deficit in energy: the level of policy energy is lower than quantum learning.

Source: Whiteshield

Now, how do these E–Q statements inform you about your risks? A positive E–Q means you will be performing worse than expected in your development goals and can face efficiency or economic tensions. A negative E–Q means you will be performing better than expected in your development goals but can face social tensions.

3.3 The Target Statements

Guided by your balance of policy and your risk assessment, the following step is to fix your targets. Targets in plural because you need a development target (the 'what' target) and an E–Q target (the 'how' target). The 'what' target is about what you want to achieve, that is how much progress on your development goals for a fixed time horizon. If your P&L statements revealed a negative development gap, you are performing worse than your potential, and the target could simply be to close the gap, but it could also be to close it and go beyond your current potential.

Your strategy to accomplish that is outlined in the E–Q target statement (Figure 45). Simply closing the gap between your potential and your realised development performance would require closing the gap between the level of energy invested and the level of quantum learning. Going beyond the current development potential requires closing the E–Q gap and further increasing both development drivers. An alternative way to look at it is via the notion of Return on Energy (ROE), which is the simple ratio between your development performance and the energy invested. Closing the gap between potential and actual development performance is about increasing the Return on Energy ratio. Holding your energy constant while increasing your potential development performance is about increasing the levels of energy invested for a constant ROE.

4. OUTLINING A PLAN

At this stage you know how much progress you want to achieve and how. The objective of this phase is to get into the specifics. Say your target statements indicate that you need to increase both your energy and your quantum learning by a certain amount in order to achieve your development targets. You need to know how specifically you can enhance your levels of energy and quantum learning. A first step in that direction is the 'P.L.A.N.I.C'.

4.1 The 'P.L.A.N.I.C'

This step assesses and outlines the actions required for each variable of the Energy and the Quantum Learning blocks in the development equation: Policy mix, Legitimacy, Administrative efficiency, Narrative, Individual meaning and Community.

Figure 45. Illustrative target statement

TARGET STATEMENTS

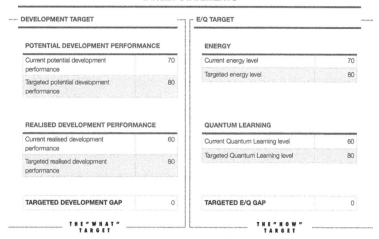

DEVELOPMENT TARGET		E/Q TARGET	
POTENTIAL DEVELOPMENT PERFORMANCE		**ENERGY**	
Current potential development performance	70	Current energy level	70
Targeted potential development performance	80	Targeted energy level	80
REALISED DEVELOPMENT PERFORMANCE		**QUANTUM LEARNING**	
Current realised development performance	60	Current Quantum Learning level	60
Targeted realised development performance	80	Targeted Quantum Learning level	80
TARGETED DEVELOPMENT GAP	0	**TARGETED E/Q GAP**	0

THE "WHAT" TARGET

- The development target sets the objective in terms of realized development performance and in terms of gap between potential development performance and realized development performance.
- In this case the target in terms of development objective is higher than the current the potential performance. The country needs to close the gap between potential and realized performance and further increase its potential.

THE "HOW" TARGET

- While the development target statement outlines the "what" objective, the E/Q statement outlines the "how" by setting the general path the country needs to follow to achieve its objective. The statement indicates targets in term of energy, quantum learning and E/Q gap.
- In this case, the country needs to both increase its energy levels and close the gap between energy and quantum learning.

GRAPHICAL REPRESENTATION TARGET STATEMENT

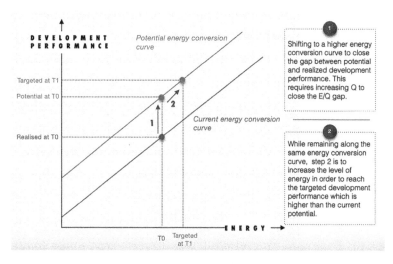

1 Shifting to a higher energy conversion curve to close the gap between potential and realized development performance. This requires increasing Q to close the E/Q gap.

2 While remaining along the same energy conversion curve, step 2 is to increase the level of energy in order to reach the targeted development performance which is higher than the current potential.

Source: Whiteshield

The policy mix:

Starting with the policy mix, the objective is to understand how your choice of policies can be improved. In order to do that, you can rely on three tools: The experience curve, the periodic table of policies and the policy opportunity matrix. The experience curve gives a first assessment of the policy mix by mapping policies according to their level of influence on the network of policy goals and their level of dependence or connectedness to other policies. It allows you to identify whether the policies you are most adopting fall at the top of the curve with a high influence and high connectedness or at the bottom of the curve. In Figure 46, the size and darkness of the bubbles indicates the adoption score of the policy. The largest and darkest bubbles are those policies that the society is adopting the most. In this case, they mostly fall in the second tier of influential policies, that is mostly economic enablers showcasing potential for improvement in adoption of the most influential, foundational policies.

The periodic table of policies gives a second-level assessment allowing you to identify what blocks of policies you are focusing on. The table classifies policies by periods, groups and blocks according to their impact and the concentration pattern of that impact (i.e. impact concentrated on a few policy issues vs spread across several policy issues).

In Figure 47, policies most adopted by the society are represented by the darker cells. We can see that they fall mainly in the top left and the bottom right of the table. The top left represents the light policies block: policies with a relatively low impact concentrated on a few policy issues. The bottom right represents the heavy policies: those with a maximum impact combined with a maximum spread over the network of policy issues. We can see that the policy mix of the society is too contrasted and we need to further enhance the adoption of policies in the intermediary blocks, which can act as connectors or targeted means of action.

Finally, the **policy-opportunity matrix** allows you to assess your policy mix against your specific priority areas. It is an answer to the following question: 'are my policies adapted to my weaknesses?' The matrix maps policies according to their level of adoption and their policy-opportunity gain. The latter is a policy and country-specific metric measuring the influence of the policy on all development goals where the country does not have a revealed comparative advantage, otherwise defined as a weakness

Figure 46.   Illustrative country experience curve

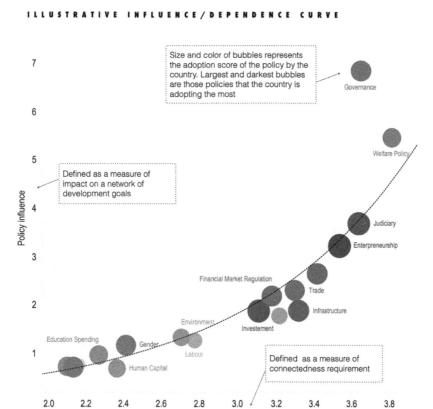

ILLUSTRATIVE INFLUENCE/DEPENDENCE CURVE

Source: Whiteshield

area. In Figure 48, there is a clear segment of policies, in a dotted-line box to the top left of the graph which have a high unexploited potential. Their policy-opportunity gain is higher than average while their adoption is lower than average.

The legitimacy:

The second variable to assess and plan for in the Energy block is your legitimacy. Every public policy can be approached as a form of contract between policymakers and individuals. This contract engages a reciprocal relationship where individuals accept to make sacrifices and pay a certain price, in exchange for what they receive from the public policy in question. This contractual relationship entails a level of trust which will be a key

Figure 47.   Illustrative country periodic table of public policies

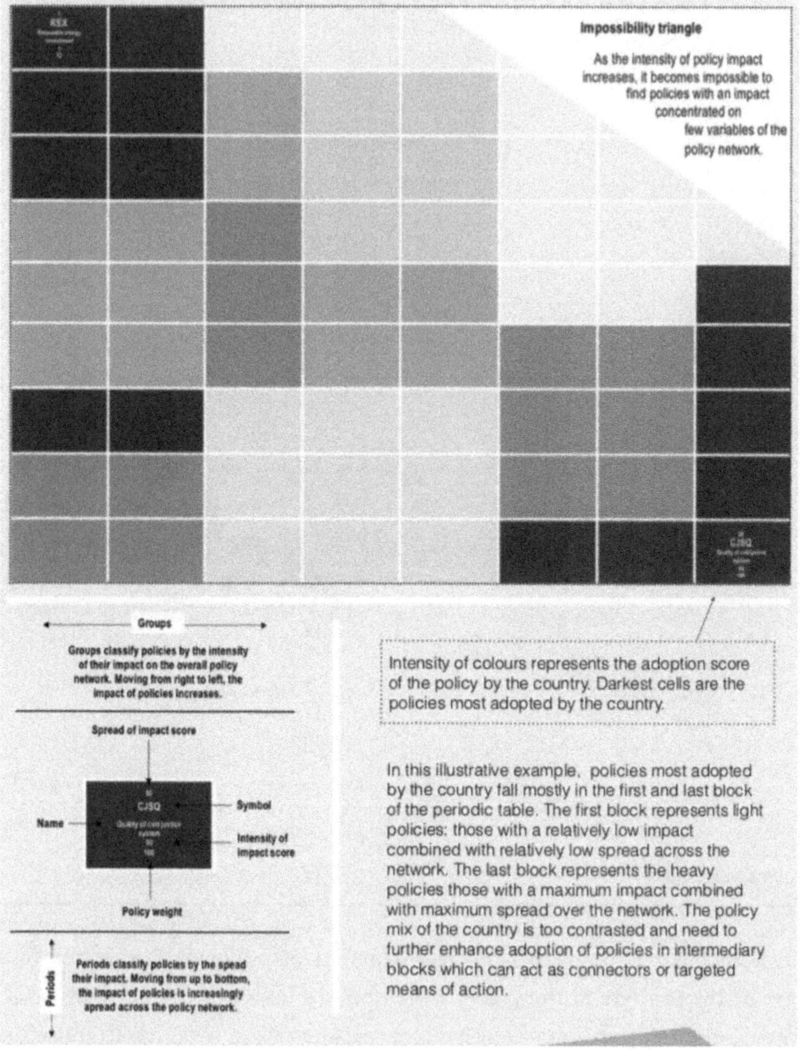

Impossibility triangle

As the intensity of policy impact increases, it becomes impossible to find policies with an impact concentrated on few variables of the policy network.

◀——— Groups ———▶

Groups classify policies by the intensity of their impact on the overall policy network. Moving from right to left, the impact of policies increases.

Spread of impact score

Name —— [C/SQ Quality of civil justice system] —— Symbol / Intensity of impact score

Policy weight

Periods classify policies by the spead their impact. Moving from up to bottom, the impact of policies is increasingly spread across the policy network.

Intensity of colours represents the adoption score of the policy by the country. Darkest cells are the policies most adopted by the country.

In this illustrative example, policies most adopted by the country fall mostly in the first and last block of the periodic table. The first block represents light policies: those with a relatively low impact combined with relatively low spread across the network. The last block represents the heavy policies those with a maximum impact combined with maximum spread over the network. The policy mix of the country is too contrasted and need to further enhance adoption of policies in intermediary blocks which can act as connectors or targeted means of action.

Source: Whiteshield

determinant of your ability to enact your strategies. Indeed, holding high levels of trust can be a strong accelerator for policymaking by reducing transaction costs, enhancing compliance, improving enforcement and strengthening the power of narratives.

Figure 48.   Illustrative country policy-opportunity matrix

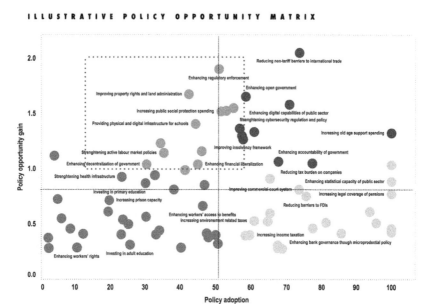

Source: Whiteshield

As such, levels of trust need to be assessed and monitored continuously and actions to nurture trust included in every policy strategy. To do so, you need to look at three main factors (Figure 49).

Firstly, there are the trustees. Here, the idea is to understand to what extent the legitimacy varies between the 'system', the government and the administration in order to identify where to focus your actions.

Secondly, there are the drivers. Here, careful attention should be given to the drivers of trust, or lack thereof. More specifically, two types of trust drivers can be tracked: values-driven trust and expertise-driven trust.

Finally, there are the trustors. The idea is to track the key differentiating factors in the level of trust among your target population (such as age, sex or income levels) in order to identify priority actions to increase legitimacy.

The administrative efficiency:

Following the assessment of your policy system and legitimacy, you need to assess your administrative system. This aims at answering the following question: 'do I have the required capabilities to implement my policy mix?'

Figure 49.   Illustrative country legitimacy dashboard

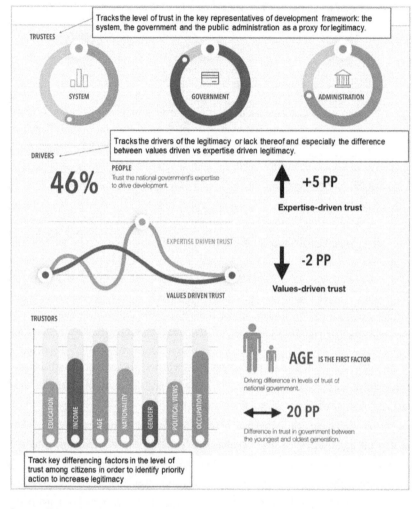

Source: Whiteshield

Capabilities can be hard to measure and identify directly. An interesting approach is the one adopted by economic complexity that measures the capabilities of a society or country by looking at the diversity and ubiquity of the products exported. In the same spirit, we argue that administrative capabilities can be inferred by looking at the diversity and uniqueness of policies, where society benefits from a revealed comparative advantage.

Figure 50 maps countries according to the complexity of their policy system and its diversity. Here, a country is considered to have a revealed comparative advantage in a policy if its adoption score is higher than the world median and higher than the predicted score given its public budget. If you have a revealed comparative advantage in a large number of policies (y-axis), and in unique policies that is ones where very few countries have a revealed comparative advantage (x-axis), it is considered to mean that you benefit from an efficient and capable administrative system (the top right quarter of the graph).

The policy narrative:

The final component of the energy analysis is the narrative. The idea here is to understand whether the communication about your policy mix is right. Your policy system has a powerful narrative if it abides by three principles (Figure 51).

Figure 50. Illustrative policy complexity matrix

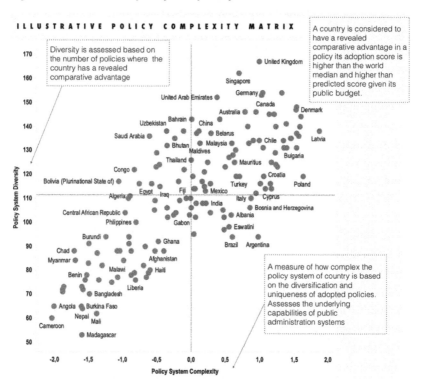

Source: Whiteshield

Figure 51.   Illustrative policy narrative spider graph

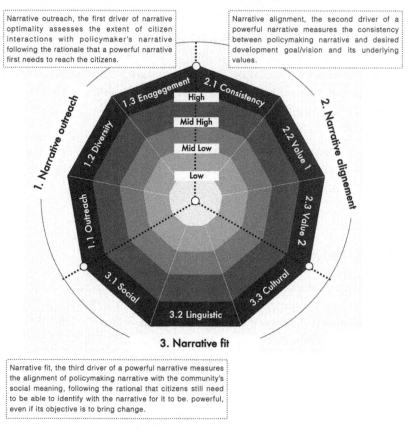

Narrative outreach, the first driver of narrative optimality assesses the extent of citizen interactions with policymaker's narrative following the rationale that a powerful narrative first needs to reach the citizens.

Narrative alignment, the second driver of a powerful narrative measures the consistency between policymaking narrative and desired development goal/vision and its underlying values.

Narrative fit, the third driver of a powerful narrative measures the alignment of policymaking narrative with the community's social meaning, following the rational that citizens still need to be able to identify with the narrative for it to be. powerful, even if its objective is to bring change.

Source: Whiteshield

Firstly, a high narrative outreach. For every communicative action, your narrative will be powerful only if a lot of people are aware of it. This represents the quantitative aspect: 'How much attention do speeches of policymakers get?', 'How often do citizens interact with policymakers via digital channels?', 'How diversified is the audience of the policy narrative?' and 'Does the narrative reflect the actual diversity of the population?'

In addition to these quantitative criteria, you need to consider two main qualitative principles. The first principle is the narrative alignment: 'How consistent is the narrative with the development vision and its underlying values?' A country aiming at SDGs as development goals aspires to be an inclusive and sustainable society and these themes need to be recurrent and highlighted in policymakers' narratives. The second principle is the narrative fit: citizens need to be able to identify with the narrative for it to be powerful and have a high impact. Even, and especially, if its objective is to bring change, the narrative still needs to leverage the common core beliefs and values of the community in order to tap into the collective meaning.

The individual meaning:

Moving to the second block of variables, the objective here is to assess the strength of individual meaning in your country, which partly conditions levels of quantum learning. Drivers of an individual's ability to absorb policies and convert them into tangible achievements are partly summarised by the sociological concept of capitals: economic, social and cultural capitals or backgrounds, which condition, to a certain extent, the habits, aspirations, motivations and actions of individuals. As such, a useful exercise at this stage is capitals segmentation (Figure 52), allowing us to understand the distribution of the three forms of capital that are driving individual meaning and how they can influence behaviour.

Figure 52.   Illustrative capital matrix

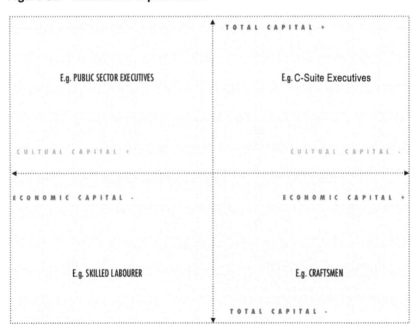

Source: Whiteshield

The community:

The final component of your plan is the community. The objective here is to understand to what extent your community, and its core beliefs and values, is aligned with your development vision, a key factor of the ability to absorb and convert the policy mix. Assessing this alignment first requires a mapping of values underlying your development goals (Figure 53).

For instance, if your development goal is to achieve SDGs, your development vision would be to nurture a sustainable, inclusive and productive society. The question to answer is, if your community were to be fully aligned with this vision, then what beliefs and values should be at the core of its social meaning (Figure 54).

Following this exercise of mapping your core development values, you need to assess their alignment with your community. You can think of the community as three levels of depth (Figure 55). The deepest level is the community meaning: the fundamental shared convictions, values and beliefs at the core of your collective social meaning. These are conditioned by the second level, community drivers: the set of socio-cultural factors shaping the meaning. They include the language, the religion, the cults, the ethnicity and

Figure 53.   The three layers of development goals

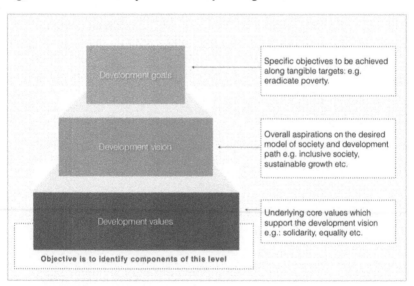

Development goals — Specific objectives to be achieved along tangible targets: e.g. eradicate poverty.

Development vision — Overall aspirations on the desired model of society and development path e.g. inclusive society, sustainable growth etc.

Development values — Underlying core values which support the development vision e.g.: solidarity, equality etc.

Objective is to identify components of this level

Source: Whiteshield

Figure 54. Example of mapping of sociocultural values associated with the development goals

Socio-cultural value	Definition	Development orientation
Power Distance	Centralisation is popular. Inequalities between people are both expected and desired, privileges and status symbols are both expected and popular.	Low power distance High power distance
Individualism	Individual forms the basis for identity, opinions expressed openly, achieving individual goals is more important than interpersonal relationships, low- context communication.	Collectivism Individualism
Uncertainty Avoidance	Fear of the ambiguous and unknown. What is different is dangerous. Suppression of deviant ideas and behaviour; resistance to innovation.	High appetite for risk Uncertainty avoidance
Masculinity	Material success and progress, money and things are important, as well as equity, competition among colleagues, performance, conflicts can be resolved by confrontation	Femininity Masculinity
Materialism	Strong emphasis on material needs and physical and economic security.	Post-materialism Materialism
Pragmatism	Encouraging thrift and efforts in to prepare for the future which is more important than maintaining time-honoured traditions and norms.	Normativism Pragmatism
Indulgence	Weak control of socialisation processes on individuals' desires and impulses. Strong emphasis on leisure time and gratification of desires.	Restraint Indulgence

Source: Whiteshield

the identity. They are more visible than the community meaning. Finally, the third level covers the most visible aspects of the community: the artefacts which include symbols, stories, myths, rituals, practices, behavioural patterns, and tangible cultural elements.

As such, the exercise becomes an analysis of this third level of community artefacts through the different community drivers, in order to assess the alignment of inferred social meaning with the core development values

Figure 55.   The three layers of the community

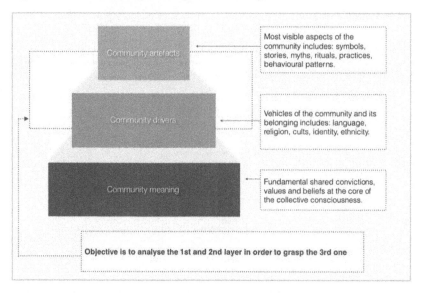

Community artefacts

Most visible aspects of the community includes: symbols, stories, myths, rituals, practices, behavioural patterns.

Community drivers

Vehicles of the community and its belonging includes: language, religion, cults, identity, ethnicity.

Community meaning

Fundamental shared convictions, values and beliefs at the core of the collective consciousness.

Objective is to analyse the 1st and 2nd layer in order to grasp the 3rd one

Source: Whiteshield

established previously and identify key areas of action for your community plan (Figure 56).

4.2 The Policy Plans

Following the first level of planning along the various variables of the development equation, a second step is needed before reaching an actional roadmap. This second step conducts the 'P.L.A.N.I.C' exercise at the policy level rather than the country level. It starts with an identification of the most problematic policy challenges (Figure 57). The identification is based on the experience curve introduced earlier. A policy will be considered problematic if its positioning along the country's curve is different from the expected theoretical positioning, which would indicate a lower-than-expected return on energy for that specific policy. Once the policy has been identified, an assessment for that specific policy of the challenges along the six variables of the equation is needed in order to further narrow down areas of action.

Figure 56.   Illustrative assessment of the alignment between the community and the development vision

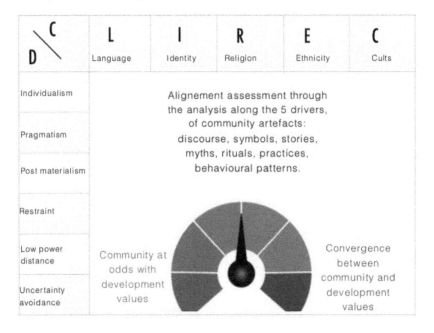

Source: Whiteshield

4.3 The National Agenda

The final step is to translate the 'P.L.A.N.I.C' and the policy plans into a national agenda outlining a set of key actions to achieve the targets set in the strategy. More specifically, three plans need to be derived: the policy plan, the administrative plan and the communication plan. These are the three areas of actions where the policymaker has the actual power to make a change. However, the actions included should cover responses to the challenges along the six different variables of the equation.

5. IMPLEMENTING THE PLAN

Guided by your national agenda the final step is to implement it. While the details of an implementation plan will vary depending on the details of the agenda, a common set of principles can be outlined.

Figure 57.   Steps of the P.L.A.N.I.C exercise at the policy level

1. Identification of the policy challenge

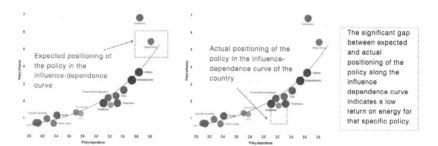

2. Diagnostic of the policy challenge

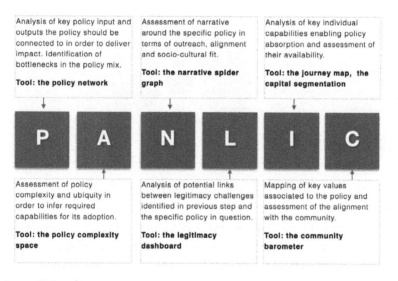

Source: Whiteshield

Firstly, policymakers and public administrations are part of the quantum learning. Their absorption capacity matters and needs to be enhanced as well. A change in public policy frameworks or strategies is in itself a policy and one that cannot be successful if individuals are not enabled to absorb it and convert it into tangible achievements. This requires changing the educational approach to public policy. The academic world is certainly not immune to this issue. Public policy, political studies and policy studies, were once connected fields but have now become divergent. Policy studies have evolved over the past fifty years towards an analysis-centric framework with a strong, and sometimes exclusive, focus on technical expertise and quantitative evaluation methods which have become the very subject of these studies. It is fundamental to ensure an effective cross-disciplinary approach to teaching public policy and infuse complex thinking to bridge the gap between the theory and reality of policymaking.

Secondly, act in networks, not silos. The key unit of action is the individual and network of individuals. This is also true for policymakers and administrations themselves. Maintaining bureaucratic barriers around administrative silos is not aligned with the complex reality of interconnected policy areas. Governance structures should also evolve towards a network-based organisation with effective coordination and utilisation of a whole-of-country approach.

Thirdly, do not monitor new strategies with outdated metrics. The metrics we choose have considerable impact on the success or failures of strategies. Attempting to use a new framework, a new strategy while monitoring progress with metrics of the past will be useless. An effective change of strategies can only happen if all social organisations involved develop and adopt metrics to measure what is targeted by the strategy. A key example is the individual absorption capacity and its drivers. In general, human capital metrics need to be improved to account for the actual capabilities of individuals rather than proxies such as educational achievements. A change of metrics is also needed in other key dimensions, such as systematic quantification of linkages between policy fields to effectively break down silos and incentivise coordination between public policy sectors, or more advanced metrics to assess the intangibles of change, including social cohesion and informal institutions.

Fourthly, individualisation is possible. The flaws of the 'one size fits all' mindset have become common knowledge. Our framework only stresses, even more, the need to take the individual as the key unit of analysis and action. This means the design of policies mindful of individual differences, targeted policy delivery or targeted narratives. While this might not have been feasible decades ago, leveraging the digital tools at hand certainly makes it a less arduous task now. If product design can be centred around user journeys, if products can be customised, and if an online advertisement can be tailored to different profiles, surely policy systems can also move along that direction.

CONCLUSION

Policymakers are still operating under a sectoral framework based on linear thinking, structured around abstract policy silos, and restricted to the realm of policymaking.

In the previous four chapters, we have established the limitations of the current system, and now it is time to address how to change our thinking. This quantum development framework points to the need for a paradigm change in policymaking. Policymakers around the world are still operating under a sectoral framework based on linear thinking, structured around abstract policy silos, and restricted to the realm of policymaking.

Accelerating progress in SDGs and development goals, in general, requires transitioning to a policy network framework which consciously leverages the linkages between the various policy fields in order to achieve multidimensional but integrated development goals. But even more importantly, a leap towards a quantum governance paradigm is required to internalise the social and human factors of sociotechnical systems in the policymaking process and move beyond the narrow focus on the policy instruments toward a one-to-one citizen-centric model.

1. BRING BACK FUNDAMENTAL QUESTIONS

Fundamental questions should be considered as a check and balance mechanism. In a detail-oriented policy paradigm with a high focus on technical instruments, broad conceptual questions might seem counterproductive, unnecessary or even useless, but their importance should not be underestimated. Reinstating a habit of questioning assumptions taken for granted and core mechanisms considered as mainstream and unchangeable should be a top priority in the public policy realm. Questions should be asked such as: 'What is the direction we are headed towards as a society', 'What is development', 'What is a public policy', 'What is a job', etc. The objective is threefold. Firstly, it is to avoid misguided policy interventions and the far too-common pitfall of analogy thinking. We are at a stage in public policy where technical instruments are decontextualised, packaged as best practices inspired by the experience of successful examples worldwide, and chosen by analogy. It is almost as if we could talk about a peer-pressure phenomenon in public policy, the pressure of introducing a policy because it has been adopted widely or has led to conclusive results elsewhere, despite significant contextual differences. Secondly, it is to escape closed debates. The 'how' questions which dominate public policy inherently frame policy interventions within a realm of narrow options subject to various cognitive biases such as the confirmation, the commitment or the availability biases. Using fundamental questions as a check and balance system allows us to broaden this horizon of policy options, and consider the possibility that we are not asking the right questions rather than not choosing the right answer. They allow us cognitive shifts to connect issues which were thought to be separate. Finally, it is to spur innovation within public policy. Answers are a finite game and thinking by analogy can only lead to recycling those answers. Enhancing creativity in public policy requires admitting that sometimes we simply lack answers that still work and that we need to go back to the fundamental questions.

2. FOCUS ON THE CONSTANTS OF CHANGE

When considering a story of change, our instinct is to focus on precisely what changed, on the differences between the past and the present or between place A and place B, the differences in the space–time continuum. This leaves us with descriptive narratives specific to a certain context and which cannot help us derive well-founded insights for other contexts. The narrative of the first Industrial Revolution did not replicate itself during the second or third revolutions and the regions that tried to replicate the 'key ingredients' of Silicon Valley more often than not failed to do so. What we should focus on

instead of the narratives are the constants: despite structural transformations, what is it that remained unchanged? The objective is to derive first
principles which represent the core fundamentals that can be found in any
change story. A common framework, a common mind map, a common trans-
lation tool that should represent the building blocks of public policy and
development. Every social organisation, be it an empire, a country, a city, a
neighbourhood or something else, is motivated by a common goal. The public policy system includes the rules, institutions and narratives put in place to
constrain or channel individual behaviour towards that common goal. On
the receiving end of this policy system is a network of individuals motivated
not only by their own interest, ambition and beliefs, but also by common values cemented by the community. The building block of any change story, of
any development narrative, is the interaction between this system of public
policies and the network of individuals which shapes the progress of social
organisations towards their common goal. As such, understanding, assessing, quantifying and tracking that interaction should be the purpose of our
analytical frameworks to guide public policy systems in the achievements of
common goals.

3. RECOGNISE THAT NO SYSTEM IS ETERNAL

The most dangerous aspect of a system is for it to become so entrenched
in assumptions raised to the standard of absolute truth that it is no longer
capable of real change, and of admitting those assumptions are not valid
anymore. That is when thinking becomes ideology. This represents the highest obstacle to resilience, self-regeneration and spontaneous adaptation. History is not short of examples of the fall of powerful systems perceived by
their contemporaries as eternal. This humbling lesson that historical hindsight brings should be a guiding principle of public policy and is all the more
fundamental and relevant for our current policy systems. Indubitably, we are
witnessing an era of structural transformation, but one where convergence is
missing. That is convergence between the 3rd and 4th ages of development.
On the one hand, there are policy systems which are still deeply rooted in an
'optimisation' mindset characteristic of the 3rd age of development with a
strong focus on economic growth, profit maximisation and competition for
resources. And on the other hand, there are individual and societal meanings

shifting towards the 4th age of development based on decentralisation of power and trust, transition to collaborative networks, new policy prioritisation and all in all higher absorptive capacity for the network of individuals powered by technological disruptions. Currently, there is a divergence visible in an increasing policy cynicism, a development glass ceiling and decreasing social cohesion. For policy systems to be resilient in these critical times, it is more important than ever to remind ourselves of the perishability of once dominant paradigms and to question assumptions which have been taken for granted for far too long in the public policy realm.

4. IMPLEMENT EXPIRATION DATES FOR PUBLIC POLICIES

The same point highlighted in the preceding section is valid at a lower level, for individual policies, laws or institutions. Our modern civilisations are characterised by an incredibly high amount of complexity which is understandable and required given the extent of the challenges to solve. However, that becomes a threat when returns on complexity are diminishing. That is when an increase in complexity to deal with societal requirements does not help solve as many challenges as it used to. One element that does not help mitigate this threat is the accumulative nature of our policy and administrative systems: laws adding to existing laws, institutions founded on top of existing ones, etc. This is directly related to our perception of policy and institutional systems. It is a misleading perception that they are supposed to last for a long period of time, if not forever. However, any public intervention, be it a policy, law or institution, effectively, has an expiration date when individual absorption capacity for said intervention starts decreasing, and when individual and social meaning are not aligned with it anymore. The ability to recognise this effective expiration date and in turn institutionalise it is critical.

5. ALLOW FOR ANALYTICAL FLEXIBILITY IN SPATIO-TEMPORAL UNITS

The rhythm of development and progress is often illustrated by continuous, incremental and steady sweeping curves allowing for a clear distinction between short-, medium- and long-term horizons. However, it is fundamental to keep in mind that, as is the case for any complex system or complex process, there is room for sudden events, tipping points and reversals. Indeed, policymaking can appear stable for long periods, only to be destabilised profoundly. Most policies can stay the same for long periods while a small number change quickly and dramatically. Or, policy change in one issue may be minimal for decades, followed by profound change which sets policy on an entirely new direction. This has two main implications. Firstly, it makes the tracking of quantum learning by policy systems all the more critical because even though its drivers, individual and social meaning, might seem prone to long-term continuous evolutions rather than sudden ones, the latter can still happen. For instance, a sudden evolution can happen, when segments of individuals with different individual meanings suddenly have convergent interest, via an awakening of the community on a specific issue, or simply if the gap between the energy of the policy system and the quantum learning becomes so high that a tipping point is reached. Secondly, it is necessary to approach time horizons with flexibility and caution, since framing a particular issue as a long-term one can prevent us from foreseeing patterns of sudden change and potential shorter-term tipping points.

A similar analytical flexibility should govern policy frameworks regarding spatial units. The transition in the geographical scale of issues from local to regional, national, supranational and global is becoming significantly more fluid. Yet, a methodological nationalism is still far too common. Methodological nationalism assumes that the nation-state and society are the natural social and political forms of the modern world. It assumes that humanity is naturally divided into a limited number of nations, which on the inside organise themselves as nation-states, and on the outside set boundaries to distinguish themselves from other nation-states. And this analytical issue inherently equates the spatial unit of policy interventions with this national frame of reference making the consideration of other units, more relevant in certain cases, a less spontaneous and systematic one.

6. DESACRALISE THE GROSS DOMESTIC PRODUCT (GDP) METRIC

We owe the premise of the GDP to US economist Simon Kuznets and its modern version to British economist John Maynard Keynes who in 1940 was attempting to measure the production capabilities of the UK in times of war. Four years later, the Bretton Wood Conference sealed the use of GDP as the ultimate metric to measure country development. And that forged an economy-centric narrative of development, one that simply equates development with economic development. The debate on the shortcomings of GDP is certainly not a new one. In 1968, US politician Robert Kennedy was already proclaiming in his famous election speech, that 'GDP measures everything in short, except that which makes life worthwhile'. The challenge of using better alternative metrics is becoming a pressing one, for two mains reasons.

Firstly, the expanding gap between, on the one hand theoretical development goals and narratives, and on the other the persisting prioritisation of GDP as the ultimate development and policy metric. In 1998, Indian economist Amartya Sen was awarded the Nobel Prize in Economic Sciences for his work on human capabilities and his innovative approach to development stating that it should be assessed via its actual impact on individuals' lives and understood as the continuous process of expanding their ability to 'be and do desirable things in life': being healthy, going to school, working, etc. He paved the way for the notion of Human Development which came to life with the Human Development Index and the Multidimensional Poverty Index. This initiated a general movement of finding alternative metrics to assess development and a proliferation of multidimensional indices attempting to encompass all aspects of development from economic to social and environmental dimensions. It also led to a reconsideration of subjective measures of well-being under the assumption that the role of development, the mission of societies, is to promote individual happiness or as Aristotle would say 'flourishing lives'. However, and despite this diversification in development metrics, no compelling alternative managed to rise to the standard of GDP in the public policy world. One might wonder why that matters. If policy systems are effectively prioritising other development goals, does it matter if GDP still benefits as a metric from a global importance? The answer is yes. For the tyrannical power of metrics should not be underestimated. In quantum physics, the observer effect says that the mere act of observing an experiment will necessarily alter it. That is also true of social and human phenomena. The reality of the development of countries undeniably changes depending on the instruments we choose to measure it. The institutionalisation of specific cognitive infrastructures or 'devices' inherently leads to seeing policy objects from a particular perspective. GDP, the same as any other metric, is not neutral and prioritising it still frames policy intervention towards a certain direction which can be in direct conflict with new development goals. The focus on GDP inherently diverts attention from key policy issues. such as distributional considerations and inequality or environmental impacts.

Secondly, even if we confine GDP's importance to the economic policy realm and equally prioritise other metrics related to priority policy goals beyond economic growth, significant challenges still remain given that GDP is vastly becoming an outdated metric unable to reflect structural transformations in the digital economy. GDP was developed during the industrial age. It was tailored for an economic paradigm where physical capital prevailed and struggles to account for today's intangible assets – services, insights, and networks. Several digital goods and services go largely uncounted in GDP because the measure is based on the price of goods and services. If something has a price of zero, then it typically contributes zero to GDP, and since the metric only accounts for how much we pay for things not how much we benefit, it does not reflect the consumer's economic well-being, the consumer surplus. This is an issue of major importance given the exponentially increasing value that customers can derive from free digital products. As US economist Robert Solow said: 'we see the digital age everywhere except in the GDP statistics'. And as long as GDP is relied upon to guide major policy decisions such as investments in infrastructure, R&D, education, cyberdefence, and regulation of the tech sector, then effectively those policies are built on a misleading metric for the digital age.

7. ADOPT NEW METRICS AND TOOLS TO TRACK INTANGIBLES

Stemming from the lack of suitable metrics, an effective change of direction to focus on quantum learning can only happen if social organisations develop and adopt metrics to measure individual absorption capacity and its drivers. In general, human capital metrics need to be improved to account for the actual capabilities of individuals rather than proxies such as educational achievements. A change of metrics is also needed in other key dimensions such as systematic quantification of linkages between policy fields to effectively break down silos and incentivise coordination between public policy sectors or more advanced metrics to assess the intangibles of change, including social cohesion and informal institutions. Technological disruptions undoubtedly bring extra layers of complexity for measurement systems, but they also bring new, powerful tools of data generation and analysis that should be fully leveraged to produce meaningful metrics.

8. REFORM MINISTRIES TO TRANSITION FROM GOVERNMENT TO NETWORKED GOVERNANCE

The key unit of action is the individual and forming a network of individuals. This also true for policymakers and administrations themselves. Maintaining bureaucratic barriers around administrative silos is not aligned with the complex reality of interconnected policy areas. And adopting a citizen-centric policy framework cannot effectively happen without citizen-centric governance. Administrative structures should also evolve towards a network-based organisation with the effective coordination and utilisation of a whole-of-country approach.

It is necessary to accept that our modern bureaucracies can and should be questioned down to their core fundamentals. The standard organisation of ministries or governmental departments might seem intuitive to us but that is mostly because centuries of existence have helped it become deeply rooted in the political imaginary. A critical thinking process is required to recognise that organisation via segregation along a series of policy domains – economy, education, labour, etc. – which are inherently connected, is born out of convenience, the accumulation of centuries of knowledge specialisation, and the progressive inclusion of new fields in public policy interventions. Attempts to break out of the reductionist organisation of public administration already exist. Whole-of-government approaches have existed since the 1990s. However, they are still considered as exceptional time-bound governance mechanisms dedicated to specific challenges. And as long as we see them as specific instruments to mobilise here and there, rather than a business-as-usual norm, the silo administrations will prevail and coordinating tasks will be relegated to newly created bodies or agencies specifically dedicated to that purpose, which only exacerbates the problem by increasing redundancy. As such, we should not be afraid of considering radical structural transformations in our public administration systems, ones that would actually enable a paradigm shift. Saying that a major reform is needed in the organisation of bodies as important as ministries or governmental departments should no longer be controversial.

More specifically, a twofold reform should be a priority. Firstly, in the horizontal division of ministries and secondly in the vertical organisation within ministries. Dividing ministries by policy domain is not compatible with 21st-century challenges and a citizen-centric policy framework. Policy domains simply represent an aggregation of tools more or less related to the same field and not goals in themselves. To enable a full alignment with a common societal vision, ministries should be organised along actual missions and objectives directly related to the empowerment and lives of citizens within the framework of said vision. To achieve its mission, each ministry would have to mobilise policies across the board of policy domains given the high linkages that exist between them. Each ministry would have to be perceived as node within a larger network of other ministries that are also mobilising policies from the same pool of policy domains, and thus inherently raising coordination and alignment to the standard of necessary requirement rather than exceptional strategy. Secondly, within ministries, the top-down vertical hierarchy is in dire need of reform after it has become clear that it no longer fits the needs of 21st-century policymaking. The same networked governance should be adopted and centred around the citizen with three main features: a citizen-centric vision across the process of policy design, implementation and delivery, a citizen-segmentation at the core of the organisational structure rather than a departmental division, and an empowerment of employees at all levels, even the junior ones, with the authority and accountability to make decisions that are in the best interests of the end-user, the citizen. Obviously, a networked governance approach should fully leverage technological tools and digital networks but relying exclusively on those while keeping a traditional organisational structure cannot enable a real paradigm shift nor an effective use of those technologies.

9. FULLY LEVERAGE POLICY NARRATIVES

Narratives and communication are too often underestimated even though they can be powerful instruments of change if outreach is maximised, and the narrative is adapted to cultural and social contexts. It is imperative to leverage new technologies to better design narratives and customise them at the individual level, to improve outreach and delivery, analyse changes in social behaviour and informal institutions in more detail, and engage in a feedback loop to adjust communications accordingly.

10. REFORM PUBLIC POLICY EDUCATION

Current public policy curriculums are also impacted by the silos to which the academic world is certainly not immune. Public policy, political studies, policy studies – all these once-connected fields have now become divergent. Policy studies have evolved over the past fifty years towards an analysis-centric framework with a strong, and sometimes exclusive, focus on technical expertise and quantitative evaluation methods which have become the very subject of these studies. It is fundamental to ensure an effective cross-disciplinary approach to teaching public policy and infuse complex thinking to bridge the gap between the theory and reality of policymaking.

GLOSSARY

Absorption capacity: this relates to the interaction of individuals with public policies and describes their ability to convert said policies into tangible achievements.

Administrative efficiency: this refers to the capabilities of public administration systems and, more specifically, to their ability to implement and deliver diverse and complex public policies. Administrative efficiency is the third variable of the Energy block in the quantum development equation and is considered to be a policy energy multiplier.

Administrative learning curve: this describes the stages that administrative systems go through when improving their capabilities by leveraging institutional memory and experimental learning.

Balance of Policy: a public accounting system that measures the development of countries and individuals beyond the focus on production and GDP. The Balance of Policy includes two entries. The policy output entry measures performance in key development and policy goals such as the Sustainable Development Goals. The policy input entry measures performance in the two main blocks of the quantum equation of development, that is the Energy block and the Quantum Learning block.

Block: in the periodic table of public policies, blocks group public policies which are unified in terms of their influence on the policy network and the concentration of said influence across the network. The table includes six blocks ranging from the low impact, low concentration block to the high impact, high concentration block.

Civilisational age: this refers to a stage of the development of civilisations and describes the dominant societal system during said stage. Each system includes a dominant societal direction (i.e. what are societies trying to achieve? what is their core mission?), a development paradigm, an economic paradigm and a set of features such as the frequency of disruptions, the management of resources and their surplus, and the dominant voice of guidance in development.

Community: this represents the set of shared informal institutions, beliefs, values and norms which unite a network of individuals. These norms, also referred to as the social meaning, are shaped by community drivers which include the language, the religion, the cults, the ethnicity and the identity and manifest themselves in community artefacts such as symbols, myths, artistic productions and customs.

Dependence: also referred to as systemic dependence, this is a policy network metric. Each public policy 'x' of the network has a systemic dependence score. This score is the sum of the influence of all other policies and policy outcomes included in the network on the policy 'x'.

Development paradigm: this defines the 'north' of policymaking by providing a framework for what development is supposed to be in terms of tangible objectives.

Development path: this describes the trajectory followed by countries in the progress towards their policy objectives, depending on the gap between the two blocks of the quantum equation of development: the Energy and the Quantum Learning blocks.

Energy block: this is the first block of the quantum equation of development and focuses on policy systems and aggregate-level interventions intended to channel or constrain individual behavior in order to enable the achievement of common development goals. It is defined as the momentum out into the world by policymakers through policies, formal institutions, narratives and legitimacy systems.

Energy multiplier: this refers to three out of the four variables of the Energy block: legitimacy, administrative efficiency and policy narrative. These variables are described as energy multipliers because they can enhance or reduce the initial amount of energy introduced by technical instruments included in the policy mix.

Energy path: this refers to the development path followed by countries where the policy energy is significantly higher than the quantum learning. It is characterised by relatively slow progress in development goals due to a lag effect, but a high social cohesion.

Experience curve: the experience curve plots public policies on a graph depending on their systemic influence and systemic dependence scores. It describes the role played by public policies in the policy network where each policy instrument and each policy goal are considered as a node of the network. The position of a public policy in the experience curve depends on several factors including factors inherent to the policy instrument in question and factors related to the time and experience in dealing with the policy and integrating it into the policy network. The experience curve showcases three main stages of policy experience: a slow experience stage where an increase in policy dependence is associated with a lower than proportional increase in influence, a rapid experience stage where an increase in policy dependence is associated with a higher than proportional increase in policy influence, and finally an experience glass ceiling depicting a saturation of policy integration efforts.

Group: in the periodic table of public policies, a group refers to the horizontal categories that arrange public policies by their influence on the overall policy network. There are six groups in the table ranging from minimal influence on the policy network, to maximal influence.

Habitus: this refers to the socially ingrained habits, skills and dispositions of individuals. These dispositions are shaped by the various capitals of individuals including the economic capital, the social capital and the cultural capital.

Individual meaning: this refers to the abilities, aspirations and motivations of individuals as conditioned by their immediate background (economic, social and cultural capitals) and their unique quality.

Individual path: this refers to the development path followed by countries where the policy energy is significantly lower than the quantum learning. It is characterised by an accelerated rate of progress towards development goals but a low social cohesion.

Influence: also referred to as systemic influence, this is a policy network metric. Each public policy 'x' of the network has a systemic influence score. This score is the sum of the dependence of all other policies and policy outcomes included in the network on the policy 'x'.

Legitimacy: this refers to the acceptance of the policy system's authority and subsequently its exercise of power as being right and justified. It is the glue that binds together the policymaking system and individuals. We consider that it includes both the legitimacy of the system in place and the specific leaders in power within that system. It is the second variable of the Energy block and is considered to be a policy energy multiplier.

Narrative: this refers to the story created by policymakers around the policy mix that they have in place and the policy goals and development vision that they are striving to achieve. The objective of a strong narrative is to mobilise the core beliefs of the community in order channel or constrain behavior and beliefs towards the policy objective in question. It is the fourth variable of the Energy block and is considered to be a policy energy multiplier.

Optimality of public policy mix: this refers to the set of technical instruments (laws, regulations and institutions) put in place by a policy system in order to achieve policy or development goals. The emphasis here is on the mix rather than individual policy instruments given the various linkages arising between traditional policy domains. The optimality of the policy mix is the first variable of the Energy block and is considered to be the vector of policy energy.

Period: in the periodic table of public policies, the period refers to vertical categories that arrange public policies by the concentration of their influence in the policy network. There are five periods ranging from low concentration of influence (i.e. influence is spread across the policy network) to high concentration of influence (i.e. the influence is not evenly distributed across the network and is concentrated on a few nodes).

Periodic table of public policies: this is a classification of the most widely used public policies in our current era. It is an alternative to the traditional classifications based on policy sectors or domains (e.g. education, employment, technology). The objective of the periodic table of public policies is to provide a more insightful categorisation of policies depending on patterns of behaviour and linkages in the policy network rather than arbitrary sectors. The periodic table classifies policies depending on two metrics: their influence on the policy network and the concentration of said influence.

Policy system complexity: this is a measure of how complex the policy mix of a country is, based on the diversification and uniqueness of adopted policies. It is considered as an indirect measure of the underlying capabilities of the administrative system.

Policy network: this is an alternative representation of the space of public policies where each policy instrument and each policy goal are nodes connected to other nodes by influence or dependence linkages.

Public policy paradigm: this refers to the dominant framework which includes the tools and instruments, both analytical and practical, mobilised by policymakers in order to fulfil policy or development goals.

Public policy system: this refers to all the aggregate-level interventions introduced by policymakers and the infrastructure on which they are based. It includes the policies themselves, institutions, the administrative system, narratives and legitimacy systems.

Quantum equation of development: this is a model depicting the relationship between performance in development goals (considered as the output) and inputs of development (more specifically, the energy and the quantum learning). The equation is based on the quantum principle of public policy and can be considered as the equivalent of a production function for the public policy world.

Quantum Governance: this is a public policy practice framework based on the insights derived from the quantum equation of development and the quantum principle of public policy. It is an individual-centric framework which relies on a bottom-up approach to policymaking. The framework includes both analytical tools such as the Balance of Policy and actual practices such as networked governance.

Quantum-empowerment path: this is the path followed by countries showcasing a balance between the Energy and the Quantum Learning blocks. It is characterised by an accelerated rate of progress towards development goals and a high level of social cohesion.

Quantum Learning block: this is the second block of the quantum equation of development focusing on the network of individuals at the receiving end of the policy energy. It is concerned with the ability of individuals to interact, absorb and convert public policies into tangible achievements. It includes individual meaning and the community as the two main drivers of this ability.

Quantum principle of public policy: this is a conceptual framework based on the first principles of development or what we also refer to as the constants of change. It is based on the idea that any social organisation has a set of common goals. Aggregate-level interventions are put in place to achieve progress along these goals. At the receiving end of these interventions is a network of individuals motivated by their own ambitions, interests and abilities and unified by shared beliefs and values. The interaction of individuals with the interventions put in place, and, more specifically, their ability to absorb them and convert them into tangible achievements is what conditions the progress towards common goals. As such, these interventions (that we refer to as the Energy block) and this ability of individuals to leverage them (that we call quantum learning) are the constants of change. The framework relies on the idea that individuals are the key conversion factor, which should be included in any development or policy reflection.

Quantum residual: in the model of the quantum equation of development, this refers to the gap between the Energy and the Quantum Learning blocks and, statistically, is the share of development performance that cannot be explained by energy performance. A positive quantum residual means a gap between the Energy and the Quantum Learning blocks in favour of the Quantum Learning block. A negative quantum residual means a gap between the Energy and the Quantum Learning blocks in favour of the Energy block. A quantum residual close to 0 means that energy and quantum learning are balanced.

Return on energy (ROE): this is a country-specific metric measuring its development gains depending on its policy energy level. It is the ratio of development performance to the energy score. It can be considered as the equivalent of the return on investment metric in the public policy world.

ENDNOTES

1. Weber, M. (1964). *The Theory of Social and Economic Organization*. T. Parsons (ed.). New York: Free Press

2. Peter, F. (2017). Political Legitimacy. *Stanford Encyclopedia of Philosophy*. E. Zalta (ed.). Stanford: Stanford University

3. World Health Organization. https://www.who.int/vaccine_safety/initiative/detection/immunization_misconceptions/en/index1.html

4. Birkhäuer, J. et al. (2017). Trust in the health care professional and health outcome: A meta-analysis. *PLoS ONE*. 12(2)

5. Murphy, K. (2004). The Role of Trust in Nurturing Compliance: A Study of Accused Tax Avoiders. *Law and Human Behavior*. 28(2) 187–209

6. Research as mentioned in: *Politico*. https://www.politico.eu/article/france-existential-pension-reform-battle-emmanuel-macron-strike-state/

7. Wzeig, D. (1996). To Return or Not to Return? Politics vs. Economics in China's Brain Drain. Hong Kong: Hong Kong University of Science and Technology

8. Padley, M. (2013). Delivering Localism: The Critical Role of Trust and Collaboration. *Social Policy and Society*. 12(3) 343–354

9. OECD. https://www.oecd.org/gov/trust-in-government.htm

10. European Commission: Eurobarometer. Accessed via: https://ec.europa.eu/commfrontoffice/publicopinion/index.cfm/Chart/index

11. Pew Research. https://www.pewresearch.org/fact-tank/2018/05/21/u-s-voter-turnout-trails-most-developed-countries/

12. OECD. https://www.oecd.org/gov/trust-in-government.htm

13. Friedman, J. (2017). Accessed via: https://www.niskanencenter.org/the-legitimacy-crisis/

14. OECD OPSI. Accessed via: https://oecd-opsi.org/innovations/informed-participation/

15. SpencerStuart. Accessed on 24 August via: https://www.spencerstuart.com/research-and-insight/ceo-transitions-2019

16. *Forbes* (2020). Accessed via: https://www.forbes.com/sites/alexledsom/2020/06/10/why-france-is-heading-for-another-showdown-over-pension-reform/#799dd5368fdb

17. Heilmann, S. (2007). Policy Experimentation in China's Economic Rise. *Studies in Comparative International Development.* 43: 1–26. Accessed via: http://citeseerx. ist.psu.edu/viewdoc/download?doi=10.1.1.1023.3162&rep=rep1&type=pdf

18. World Economic Forum. Accessed via: https://www.weforum.org/ agenda/2020/05/finlands-basic-income-trial-found-people-were-happier-but-werent-more-likely-to-get-jobs/

19. Maggetti, M. & Gilardi, F. (2016). Problems (and solutions) in the measurement of policy diffusion mechanisms. *Journal of Public Policy.* 36(1) 87–107. Accessed via: http://www.fabriziogilardi.org/resources/papers/Maggetti-Gilardi-JPP-2016.pdf

20. Compton, M & t' Hart, P. (2019). *Great Policy Successes.* USA: Oxford University Press

21. BBC. Accessed via: https://www.bbc.com/future/article/20190109-the-perils-of-short-termism-civilisations-greatest-threat

22. Butcher, K. (2015). Debasement and the decline of Rome. Warwick: University of Warwick. Accessed via: https://warwick.ac.uk/fac/arts/classics/intranets/staff/ butcher/debasement_and_decline.pdf

23. Timmins, N. (2016). Universal Credit: From Disaster to Recovery?. London: Institute for Government. Accessed via: https://www.instituteforgovernment.org.uk/ sites/default/files/publications/5064%20IFG%20-%20Universal%20Credit%20Pub-lication%20WEB%20AW.pdf

24. The World Bank (2014). Accessed via: https://www.worldbank.org/en/news/ feature/2014/11/19/un-modelo-de-mexico-para-el-mundo

25. Chilton, P. (2004). *Analysing Political Discourse: Theory and Practice.* London: Routledge

26. Burstein, P. (2016). The Impact of Public Opinion on Public Policy: A Review and an Agenda. *Political Research Quarterly.* 56(1) 29–40

27. Charteris-Black, J. (2005). *Politicians and Rhetoric: The Persuasive Power of Metaphor.* London: Palgrave Macmillan

28. Bonnefille, S. (2011). A Cognitive Rhetoric Approach to Two Political Speeches. *Anglophonia.* 15(30) 145–162

29. Lavigna, R. (2014). Why Government Workers Are Harder to Motivate. *Harvard Business Review.* Accessed via: https://hbr.org/2014/11/why-government-workers-are-harder-to-motivate

30. Storrs, L.R.Y., (2017). The Ugly History Behind Trump's Attacks on Civil Servants. *Politico Magazine.* Accessed via: https://www.politico.com/magazine/ story/2017/03/history-trump-attacks-civil-service-federal-workers-mccarthy-214951

31. London School of Economics. https://www.lse.ac.uk/News/Latest-news-from-LSE/2020/h-August-20/Stigmatising-unemployed-people-in-political-speech-and-the-media-affects-public-opinion

32. *Greater Good Magazine.* https://greatergood.berkeley.edu/article/item/ why_is_it_so_hard_to_change_peoples_minds

33. Reuters. https://www.reuters.com/article/us-brazil-election/ divisive-brazil-election-careens-into-dangerous-polarization-idUSKCN1LZ23S

34. Carnegie Endowment for International Peace. https://carnegieendowment. org/2019/10/01/how-to-understand-global-spread-of-political-polarization-pub-79893

35. BBC. https://www.bbc.co.uk/news/world-us-canada-53258792

36. BBC. https://www.bbc.co.uk/news/world-us-canada-53378439

37. *The New York Times.* https://www.nytimes.com/interactive/2020/07/17/upshot/ coronavirus-face-mask-map.html

38. Pew Research Center. https://www.journalism.org/2015/06/01/facebook-top-source-for-political-news-among-millennials/

39. UK Government. https://www.gov.uk/government/speeches/prime-ministers-speech-on-the-environment-11-january-2017

40. *The Diplomat.* https://thediplomat.com/2019/11/new-zealand-takes-the-lead-on-climate-change/

41. *Financial Post.* https://financialpost.com/commodities/mining/trudeau-tells-mining-conference-that-battling-climate-change-is-good-for-investment

42. Bourdieu, P. (1977). *Outline of a Theory of Practice.* Cambridge: Cambridge University Press

43. OECD (2018). *A Broken Social Elevator? How to Promote Social Mobility.* Paris: OECD

44. Social Mobility Commission (2017). *Time For Change: An Assessment of Government Policies on Social Mobility 1997-2017.* London: Social Mobility Commission

45. World Inequality Lab (2018). *World Inequality Report 2018.* Paris: World Inequality Lab

46. OECD (2018). *PISA 2018 Results: Combined Executive Summaries; Volume I, II & III.* Paris: OECD

47. Office for National Statistics (2020). *Health state life expectancies by national deprivation deciles, England: 2016 to 2018.* London: ONS

48. *The Balance.* Accessed via: https://www.thebalance.com/ trump-s-tax-plan-how-it-affects-you-4113968

49. Office for Standards in Education (2019). *Early years inspection handbook for Ofsted-registered provision.* London: Ofsted

50. Jaegar, M. (2010). Does Cultural Capital Really Affect Academic Achievement? Copenhagen: Centre for Strategic Research in Education (CSER)

51. OECD Statistics. Accessed via: https://stats.oecd.org/Index.aspx?DataSetCode=EAG_AL

52. Lin, N. (1999). Building a Network Theory of Social Capital. *Connections*. 22(1) 28–51

53. Lentz, B & Laband, D. (1989). Why So Many Children of Doctors Become Doctors: Nepotism vs. Human Capital Transfers. *The Journal of Human Resources*. 24(3) 396–413. Wisconsin: The Journal of Human Resources

54. Patacchini, E. (2016). Heterogeneous Peer Effects in Education. *Journal of Economic Behavior & Organization*. 134, Feb 2017, 190–227

55. ThoughtCo. https://www.thoughtco.com/collective-consciousness-definition-3026118

56. Gelman, S. & Roberts, S. (2017). How language shapes the cultural inheritance of categories. *PNAS*. 114(30) 7900–7907

57. Cialdini, R. et al. (1990). A Focus Theory of Normative Conduct: Recycling the Concept of Norms to Reduce Littering in Public Places. *Journal of Personality and Social Psychology*. 58(6) 1015–1026

58. Tankard, M. & Paluck, E. (2018). The Effect of a Supreme Court Decision Regarding Gay Marriage on Social Norms and Personal Attitudes. *Psychological Science*. 28(9)

59. Gallup. https://news.gallup.com/opinion/polling-matters/183518/five-things-learned-americans-moral-values.aspx

60. Reynolds, K. et. al. (2015). The Problem of Behaviour Change: From Social Norms to an Ingroup Focus. *Social & Personality Psychology Compass*. 9(1) 45–56

61. The Nobel Prize. https://www.nobelprize.org/prizes/economic-sciences/2017/press-release/

62. Institute for Government & Cabinet Office (2010). *MINDSPACE: Influencing behaviour through public policy*. London: Institute for Government

63. Troost, M. et al. (2019). Social norms of corruption in the field: social nudges on posters can help to reduce bribery. *Behavioural Public Policy*. 6(4) 597–624. Cambridge: Behavioural Public Policy

64. Akter, S. et al. (2012). Climate change scepticism and public support for mitigation: evidence from an Australian choice experiment. *Global Environmental Change*. 22(3) 736–745

65. Wanyama, J. et al. (2007). Belief in divine healing can be a barrier to antiretroviral therapy adherence in Uganda. *AIDS* 21(11) 1486–1487

66. Hogan, S. & Coote, L. (2013). Organizational culture, innovation, and performance: A test of Schein's model. *Journal of Business Research*. 67(8) 1609–1621

67. United Nations. https://www.un.org/en/un-chronicle/ you-can%E2%80%99t-be-what-you-can%E2%80%99t-see

68. Bell, A. et al. (2017). Who Becomes an Inventor in America? The Importance of Exposure to Innovation. London: Centre for Economic Performance (LSE)

69. Warin, P. (2016). The non take-up: definition and typologies. Paris: HAL

70. Mazet, P. (2014). Analysis of the non take-up of benefits: a public policy assessment tool 1. Brussels: HAL

71. Hernanz, V. et al. (2004) *Take-Up of Welfare Benefits in OECD Countries: A Review of the Evidence*. Paris: OECD

72. Department for Work and Pensions. (2020). *Income-related benefits: estimates of take-up: financial year 2017 to 2018*. London: Department for Work and Pensions

73. Harnisch, M. (2019). *Non-Take-Up of Means-Tested Social Benefits in Germany*. Berlin: Deutsches Institut für Wirtschaftsforschung

74. Middlesex University & BMG Research (2011). *Research to understand the barriers to take up and use of business support*. London: Department for Business, Innovation and Skills

75. Eurofound (2015). *Access to social benefits: Reducing non-take-up*. Luxembourg: Publications Office of the European Union

76. Eurofound. (2015). *Access to social benefits: Reducing non-take-up*. Luxembourg: Publications Office of the European Union

77. Ali, M. et al. (2013). *Factors affecting tax compliant attitude in Africa: Evidence from Kenya, Tanzania, Uganda and South Africa*. Norway: Chr. Michelsen Institute

78. Ranci, C & Arlotti, M. (2019). Resistance to change. The problem of high non-take up in implementing policy innovations in the Italian long-term care system. *Policy and Society*. 38(4) 572–588

79. Petruzzella, F. et al. (2017). The Impact of National Culture on Corporate Environmental Performance: How Much Does Your Origin Say About How Green You Are? *Journal of Environmental Sustainability*. 5(1) 1–24

80. Banerjee, A. et al. (2014) *The miracle of microfinance? Evidence from a randomized evaluation*. Massachusetts: NBER

81. Crépon, B. (2014). Estimating the impact of microcredit on those who take it up: Evidence from a randomized experiment in Morocco. *American Economic Journal: Applied Economics*. 7(1) 123–150

INDEX